The Infinite Feast

How to Host the Ones You Love

The Infinite Feast

How to Host the Ones You Love

RECIPES FROM THE BIG EASY... AND BEYOND

Illustrations
Marco Marella

Photography and Page Design
Brian Theis

Culinary Precision
Dana Jacobi

PELICAN PUBLISHING

New Orleans 2020

Edited by Devinn Adams
Photography, book design, and food styling by Brian Theis

The word "Pelican" and the depiction of a pelican are
trademarks of Arcadia Publishing Inc. and are
registered in the U.S. Patent and Trademark Office.

ISBN: 9781455625130
Ebook ISBN: 9781455625147

Printed in Malaysia
Published by Pelican Publishing
New Orleans, LA
www.pelicanpub.com

*This is a recipe and lifestyle book intended for entertainment. By using this book, its content, and these recipes,
you agree that you are entirely responsible for any damage or other liability associated with such use.*

*And while I've got your attention . . . Many of the recipes in this cookbook are not waistline-friendly.
Portion control and staying physically fit are highly recommended. Walk at least two miles every day!*

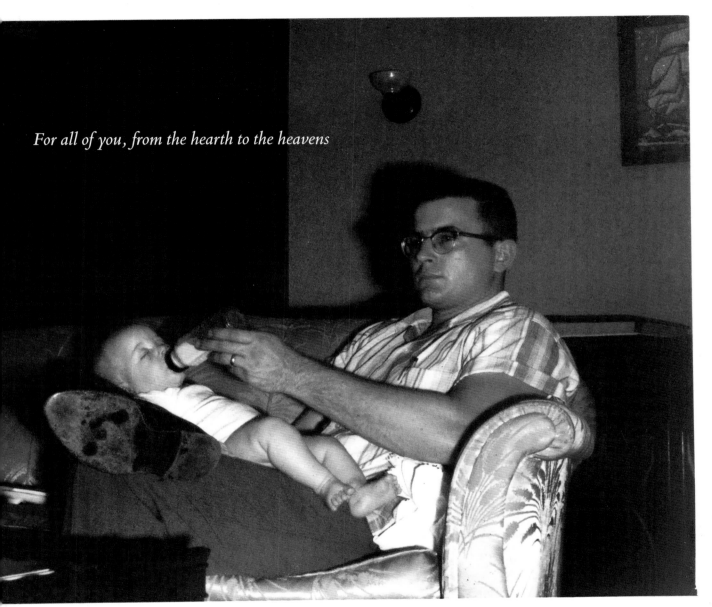

For all of you, from the hearth to the heavens

JUN • 19

Partying with Dad, Houston, Texas.

TABLE OF CONTENTS

INTRODUCTION

Cooking. Seems like everybody's doing it. It's creative. It's grounding. It's good exercise. Nice people often show up to help you. And your homemade dishes are one of the most cherished and personal gifts you can give.

Not everyone thinks cooking is for them. People say: "It takes too much organization." "I don't have the skills." "I don't have the time." "It's more effort than it's worth."

Truth be told, if you can put together a kitchen reasonably stocked with staples—salt, oil, flour, spices—and the basic tools to get started, once you get into it, you may find it *is* for you.

A lot of people talk about cooking as a calming ritual. They love the feeling of "flow" they get from losing themselves in the creation of a dish they enjoy. Like playing the violin or dancing the tango, it takes your mind off the world for an hour and gives you something to be proud of—and then eat!

People think, "My shrimp will be shocking, my salad will stink, my soufflé will be scary." Not everything is exactly right the first time you try it. Practice is good for you. If you cook it, they will come. Make it with love. You'll get love back! As I always say, you don't have to be perfect, you just have to be special.

What does special mean? Maybe you're inspired to add an ingenious twist to a favorite recipe so it becomes your signature dish. Maybe when *you* start cooking the *Friends-giving* bird, it becomes a venerable tradition and those friends wouldn't think of being anywhere else. It might mean you're a single dad and you boldly bake a pretty princess cake for your daughter's birthday that is so sweet and special you both cry happy tears together when she sees it.

Cooking at home can even save you money and make you healthier. As someone once said, (*maybe it was me?*) life is an infinite feast. Now let's kick off, shall we?!

Why I Cook

"For it is in giving that we receive."

— SAINT FRANCIS OF ASSISI

I'M a guy that's fascinated by home cooking, its techniques, and its customs. The "gateway cocktail" for me was vintage cookbooks. I have a treasured mid-century collection. Almost all of them rigorously hail from "my period," 1945 to 1965. There is a charming artistry, simplicity, and enthusiasm in the way the visuals and the methods are presented. There is always context. Who is the party for? What if company comes unexpectedly? How about *this* astonishingly-themed menu for your occasion?

I love to grocery shop. If you ask me why I cook, that's frequently the first thing that comes to mind. Going to the market is absorbing and electrifying. I love the shapes and colors and varieties of things. I spend my life in the French Quarter, Fire Island, and Greenwich Village. I grew up in Houston and San Antonio. The markets I frequent in the north, both chain and specialty, are often exceptional and chock-full to the rafters with exhilarating imports, phenomenal produce, seafood, and meats. Yet, one of the first things I do when I land in the southern states with their wide open spaces is head straight for a big name grocery. They have unique and enticing provisions as well. There's just something about a tremendous physical store with miles of aisles that gets me all fired up.

Over the past ten years, my concentration on cooking has inclined me to realize how dearly I regard the many arts it involves. These are arts I have practiced and lived. Making good food, primarily, is about appetite, learned skill, and as my Grandma Janie would say, "stick-to-it-tive-ness," but the act of producing and publishing a recipe for a home cook involves a longer list of native interests. I celebrate photography, dramatics, history, cultural identity, management, and even math when I create and cook something new. Not to mention music, and wine.

To do what I do takes everything I love doing. That's why I cook.

This book has been taking shape all my life. An early home movie shows baby Brian pulling all the pots and pans out of the cabinets. He puts a pot lid on Dad's head. Why not cook up a big batch of Dad?

Mom was clever. Kids won't eat liver. Soak it for hours in French dressing. Suddenly succulent! Mom was also the boss of sourdough pancakes and a big Texas-style pot of pinto beans.

Living with my family in The Hague, age 10, I put on a riveting three-act play, co-written with my friend Kathleen Grant. Our classmates gamely agreed to perform this epic drama in the gymnasium for the parents and teachers at our American school. Like Hitchcock did in his own films, I wrote in a fleeting cameo at the end where I played a chef. You guessed it: foreshadowing.

My first real job in life was as a busboy at a restaurant called My Place, Blanco Road and Loop 410, San Antonio. Bill and Kay Stephens owned and operated. I remember My Place affectionately, and also as a blur of never-ending Hollandaise sauce.

Then, twenty-five years ago, I fell in love with New Orleans food. Back in the day, my mother-in-law was a cooking instructor for newly-married young ladies of the city. I most adored her red beans and rice. Cousin Sistee next door was renowned for her expertise baking Lady Helen's Cheese Straws. You know what they say: when you're hot, you're hot.

I wrote and tested most of this book's 165 recipes at my home in New York City. They celebrate dishes and customs that have been around for time eternal. All generations should be glad to see these old and new friends. We begin in the winter, with its reassuring comfort food. Things progress through the seasons, via a year of rousing holidays and foreign fare. There are songs to play and parties to plan. The simplest recipes will make the purposeful cook feel accomplished, without too much complexity or stress. The main thing is being together, cooking together. It's all in the giving, as Saint Francis once said. The people you love are sure to agree.

Soon we can tuck our napkins and dig in. Deck the hallways, fill your glasses. Put those pot lids on your heads, and let's get cookin'!

—Brian Theis
New Orleans

Salt & Oil

The Grocery, the Kitchen, the Table

Gazing out over the limpid plunge pool at a riad where I'm staying at the moment in Marrakech, I'm inspired to write for you about *grocery shopping*. Just down the street from here begins the maze of souks, or markets, in the historic medina-center of Morocco's Red City. What's different about the Berber carpets, leather babouche slippers, spices, lanterns, and other notions, is that they have no price tags, one just haggles. Aside from the recommended best practices of bargaining, there are no rules.

One might say the American supermarket bears little resemblance. But every temple of commerce has its lawlessness. Just as there are no rules in Marrakech, there are plenty of schemes afoot at your local American store as well.

Things to remember, to shop better:

1. Don't cruise the aisles at eye level. Stores position products that will cost you the most money there. Instead look up and down the shelves for what's really on your list.

2. If you can avoid it, don't take the kids. All the stuff they want is at *their* eye level.

3. Your list is God. Stores move the goods around from time to time to get you to impulse buy while you search for the old location of what you really want. Outfox 'em! Stick to your list.

4. Don't go when you're hungry. Pro Tip: "duh."

5. Use a smaller shopping basket if you can, not a huge cart.

6. If one member of the family has more grocery discipline than the others, send that person.

7. Shop when nobody else will be there (e.g. early morning, church time if you're a happy pagan, or the big game if you'd rather see a musical); always use recyclable shopping bags; shop the perimeter first, that's where all the healthy and/or important stuff is; organize your shopping list by store layout and row (One of my favorite ideas—can I summon the discipline to do it? *Update: since I wrote this, I've done it!*).

8. Order everything online and have it delivered. This may be the prevailing model of the future. I identify with brick and mortar stores, as mentioned. People who shop online say they wouldn't miss real groceries or run out of ideas of what to cook if the world became virtual. I'm not sure that's true for me. *A late-breaking observation: Suddenly for the moment, as of spring 2020, home delivery is more important than ever.*

9. What to always stock? You can never have too many pimento-stuffed olives on hand. Always have a block of Parmesan cheese. At least one bottle of chilled French champagne. Sesame oil. Pasta. Frozen vegetables are not tacky. Always plan to make perfect coffee, whatever that means to you.

In New Orleans they call it… **Makin' Groceries**

A grocery in Paris

SALT

Fine salt and coarse or kosher salt

Whole black peppercorns (with a good grinder)

Chili powder

Vanilla extract

Ground cinnamon, ginger, and nutmeg

Dried oregano

Ground cumin

Smoked paprika

Garlic and onion powders

Instant diced onions (a must-have for making my famous onion dip)

Dehydrated Creole or Cajun Trinity with garlic (I use this in everything)

Cayenne pepper

Bay leaves

Fittin' in the Kitchen

If you can organize your kitchen, you can organize your life. —Louis Parrish

The Kitchen. I'll start with *supplies*. Keep yourself stocked with basic tools and versatile ingredients and you'll always be ready for action.

I conducted a social media survey recently that asked: What are the two most can't-live-without items in your pantry? I got some interesting replies. One gentleman said: peanut butter and hot sauce. That's fair. You can do a lot with those two ingredients, just ask the Indonesians. Then there was a lot of garlic, canned tomatoes, Cajun spice blends, and, of course, coffee. But the two biggies, in one form or another, were salt and oil.

In the sidebars you'll see my recommended list of pantry staples. A staple is an ingredient you keep on hand all the time, because it has a long shelf life, and it's used often. The lists are not all-inclusive of everything needed for a recipe in this book, but they're material. Following this, are your tools. Again, not exhaustive. Important to note: none of the recipes in this book require any special equipment, e.g. quesadilla maker, meat grinder, blowtorch.

Layout and Appliances. All the experts say you need a well-designed triangle between the fridge, sink, and stove. I'm not sure there's anything scientific about this other than the fact that there shouldn't be anything in your way as you move from point A to B to C. Of the three, the sink will likely get the most use, so make sure it's a size and shape you like. I've used electric and gas stoves. If I had to pick a favorite it would be gas, but I find a lot to like about the electrics as well. Fridge: I want the freezer on the bottom, fridge compartment on top. The fridge is where you go the most often so it makes sense to put it best within reach. It's also much easier to take stock of what you've got if the fridge is on top. That said, I've had freezers on the top too and it's not the end of the world.

Storage and Organization. If your kitchen has been around a while, empty all your cabinets and drawers and get rid of *everything* you don't use and/or hate. It really is okay to hate kitchen utensils. Be ruthless, but you don't need to go full Marie Kondo. Still, you must admit, the relationship you have with the broken meat thermometer your kids used as a Harry Potter wand really, truly, does not "spark joy." Now clean the insides of all said cabinets and drawers and start from scratch getting organized. It's up to you how you store frequently used pots and pans. I prefer drawers near the stove (never cabinets, too much stooping and crouching) but other folks I know of really like to hang them on the wall (Julia Child, anyone?). Put the silverware drawer near the dishwasher *and* in the direction of the dining table, if possible. Or just put it where it feels right. Along with the cooking tools drawer and the "random stuff" drawer (we all have one) it's the drawer you'll go to most.

Spices, seasonings, oils, and sauces go in an eye-level cabinet next to the stove. Spice organization is a wild card. I've put them in carefully labeled metal drawer units that sit inside a cabinet, other times I put them within easy reach in a wire rack inside a pantry door, or I sometimes put them in narrow plastic trays so I can store them in groups and just pull a tray out quickly to find what I want. Options are endless. Research online what might work best for you.

LIST OF EQUIPMENT – the roughly 30 things you need to get started

1. Chef's knife (8-inch), paring knife, serrated bread knife

2. Cast iron skillet – big one 12-inch

3. Dutch oven (5.5 to 7.25 quart) – bigger is better

4. Sheet pans – half size

5. Tongs

6. Whisk! (silicone)

7. Silicone spatulas small and flexible, large and wide – these are *essential* for getting every last bit out of a cooking vessel such as a food processor bowl or a measuring cup, so you don't leave any good bits behind

8. Large and small saucepans – 3 quart and 1 quart stainless steel – large does things like boiling and braising, small does things like sauces and gravies

9. Cutting board – wood, with "feet" on bottom so doesn't slide

10. Cotton dish towels – saves on paper! Launder them frequently.

11. Potholders and/or oven gloves

12. Nonstick skillets – large for big jobs and small for omelettes – make sure handles are oven-safe!

13. Colander and small strainer

14. Measuring cup for liquids – 2 cup measure

15. Dry measuring set – cup set and spoons – I prefer having two sets of spoons but one will do

16. Can opener – manual

17. Meat thermometer – instant read

18. *Fish* spatula – this is the most useful thing *ever*

20. Bottle opener – for vino!

21. Swivel blade vegetable peeler

22. Box grater

23. Wooden spoon

24. Slotted spoon

25. Mixing bowls – small, medium, large

26. Casserole or baking dishes – 9 x 9-inch and 9 x 13-inch – ceramic or glass

27. Parchment paper, plastic wrap, aluminum foil

28. Extra credit: electric hand mixer, kitchen shears, citrus reamer, food processor, blender, muffin tin, 9-inch pie plate, rolling pin, resealable storage containers, jar grip, zester, basting brush, small metal whisk

My kitchen, New Orleans

OIL
Olive and peanut oils
Canola, or a canola/olive blend
Toasted sesame oil
Non-stick cooking spray
Distilled white, apple cider, red wine vinegars
Soy sauce
Worcestershire sauce
Mustard: Creole, classic yellow
Mayonnaise, peanut butter

SUGAR / FLOUR
Unbleached all-purpose flour
Panko breadcrumbs
Arrowroot starch & cornstarch
Baking powder & baking soda
Cocoa powder
White & light brown sugars
Confectioners' sugar
Honey

Settin' the Table

NATIONAL HOMEMADE SOUP DAY: FEBRUARY 4

On your marks, readers! The vibe you should aim for when you're settin' the table is: "SWANKIENDA!" What the heck is swankienda, you might inquire? Well, the term was popularized by Maxine Mesinger of Houston, Texas. She wrote for the *Houston Chronicle,* and it refers to any fabulous place, whether Texan, southern, or otherwise, that is an envy-inspiring combination of swank, mid-century glamorous, and hacienda. Too tall an order? You don't have to be perfect, you just have to be special.

You want nice plates and china. I repeat: nice plates. Don't save money on the plates. A beautiful tablecloth and wonderful flatware you can save money on. Plates, not so much. Think about color. What can you collect that will suit as many seasons as possible? Will one china pattern work for spring, summer, fall, winter, New Year's, Easter, Fourth of July, Thanksgiving, Christmas? Of course it will, if you get a pattern *you* really love. If you're feeling more ambitious from a color and style standpoint, you might be able to get two flexible patterns that, in tandem,

work for all those occasions divided perfectly between holidays. Your greens are magical for Easter and Christmas, your orange for Thanksgiving and even Hallowe'en.

Silk flowers are your friend. There are so many places to get high quality ones for your table centerpieces, online and otherwise. Fresh flowers will wow your crowd the most, but silk is your standby and will never let you down. I can't recall how many times people have thought mine are real. Pro Tip: Silk flowers are like shoes, spend the money to buy the best. You will use them forever. Look for a flower arranging sidebar later in the book.

Now, for your serving ware. Later in the chapter on Mexico, I mention that you can't have too many gorgeous vintage serving trays, snack sets, and bowls. I am going to mention that essential bit of wisdom again right here.

Go to consumer-to-consumer sites that deal in collectibles to score jaw-dropping pieces that make every occasion special. (You know the sites I mean.)

The placement of the knives, forks, and spoons is important. Most of you already know the protocol there: forks on the left, appetizer fork on the outside. On the right, knives then spoons outside knives (soup spoon far right). Dessert forks and spoons go above the plate. Bread plate and knife at left, glasses at right. Look for a napkin-folding sidebar later in the book.

Above all, to have a gracious table, you must have a gracious host. Even more essential than the food you cook (which I know will be epic) . . . even more important than the food, is the tone you set, the air of calm you serenely feel (because you're so prepared), the conversation you have, and the way you love. The core principle of hosting is giving of yourself and your true *attention*. Do not forget that word. Act accordingly, and you will be the greatest host in town.

SWANK I ENDA

Stone Soup

Stone Soup is an old European folktale about decency, honesty, and giving. Its message is glad: sometimes the strangest idea (soup from a stone) can be a recipe for uniting people in a spirit of sharing. Curiosity can be the spark for fellowship, love, and cooking together. Everyone has a place at the table, including the stranger. When you give of yourself and your hospitality, spiritual wealth and lasting friendship may be your reward.

How Much Do You Already Know? Take This Cooking Quiz

1. What is the only food that will never spoil while still in an edible state?

2. Bell peppers are male if they have three lobes, or female if they have four. True or False?

3. What is the texture of pasta when you cook it al dente? Soft and delicate, or tender with a bite?

4. Tomatoes. Are they fruits, or vegetables?

5. Where did tomatoes originate: Peru, Italy, China, or Spain?

6. What ingredients do you need to make a roux? Egg whites and broth, fat and flour, or cream and wine?

7. The residue left in a pan after browning meat or sautéing vegetables is called: a) fond, brown bits, and gradoux; b) mud, crud, and schmutz; or c) roasties, toasties, and gremlins?

8. What method of flour measuring yields a greater amount of flour: spoon-and-sweep, or scoop-and-sweep? (The latter, you should know, is my method.)

9. What kind of measure should you use for sugar: liquid or dry?

10. To cut into very small cubes is to: dice, julienne, or chop?

11. What temperature should you cook chicken to? 120°F, 165°F, or 200°F?

12. How many cups, and ounces, are in a quart? 4 and 32, or 8 and 36?

13. Which is more healthy: canola oil or vegetable oil?

14. A Creole or Cajun mirepoix, also known as a trinity, is made up of: a) carrots, celery, and onion; b) bell pepper, onion, and celery; or c) raspberries, blueberries, and dingleberries?

15. What part of the pig does pork butt come from: a) ribs; b) butt; c) shoulder; or d) curlicue?

ANSWERS

1. HONEY 2. Fun, but FALSE 3. TENDER WITH A BITE 4. BOTH 5. PERU 6. FAT AND FLOUR 7. a) FOND, BROWN BITS, GRADOUX 8. SCOOP-AND-SWEEP, aka DIP-AND-SWEEP 9. DRY MEASURE 10. DICE 11. 165°F 12. 4 and 32 13. CANOLA 14. b) BELL PEPPER, ONION, CELERY 15. c) SHOULDER

HINTS 4 HUNKERING

Blizzards, power outages, tropical storms. It pays to be ready. You never know when you might have to stay inside for a while. From an unexpected pause to a lengthy lockdown.

Fill your pantry with lots of reliable dry items that are flexible, even festive

Popcorn for movie-watching
Plenty of water, other beverages
Coffee, fully stocked bar, if you imbibe
Pasta, pasta sauce, rice, dried beans, salsa
Canned tomato: whole, diced, paste
Canned vegetables, potatoes, fruit
Canned fish, tuna, sardines, meats
Jarred pickles, ketchup, mayo, jams
Broth, stock, soup & chili needs
Bread, yeast, flour, baking needs
Snacks: cookies, chips, energy bars
Cereal, granola, oatmeal
Baby food, pet food
Cake, cookie, pastry-making items
Peanut butter and chocolate!

Stock up your freezer with bedrock basics and tasty standalone standards

Hamburger, ground turkey, meatballs
Steaks, pork chops, chicken parts
Bacon, hot dogs, smoked ham
Shrimp, crab, crawfish, andouille sausage
White fish, tuna steaks, salmon fillets
Vegetables: broccoli, spinach, corn, beans
Fruit: mango, peaches, bananas, berries
Bread, butter, waffles, pancakes, biscuits
Broth, chili, pasta sauce, soup, tortillas
Frozen dinners, lasagna, pizza
Nuts: walnuts, pecans, almonds
Ice cream, pastry, pies, cookie dough
Remember: Frozen foods don't keep their quality forever. Search online: "FDA freezer storage chart" for guidance.

Make freezer-friendly dishes from this book. Cook x 2, freeze the rest!

Spicy Split Pea Soup, *25* — **Three Lime Chili,** *32* — **Hot-and-Sour Soup,** *45* — **Fried Rice,** *50* — **Flamiche (Vegetable Tart),** *64* — **Polpette (Meatballs and Sauce),** *72* — **Ragù alla Bolognese,** *77* — **Pirate Alley Gumbo,** *85* — **Hot Dog Jambalaya,** *89* — **Pimento Cheese,** *108* — **Pinto Beans,** *172* — **Bayou Stew,** *183* — **Chocolate Spider Pie,** *184* — **Mock Turtle Soup,** *187* — **Creole Crawfish 'n Cornbread Dressing,** *193* — **Apple Pandowdy,** *198* — **Christmas Party Meatballs,** *205* — **Perfect Buckeyes,** *214*
Note: Cover and seal food tightly before freezing. Thaw frozen foods in the fridge, not on counter, 6-8 hours per pound.

Essentials to have on hand for snowstorms and other social disruptions

Toilet paper, paper towels
Extra prescription medications
Pain and stomach relievers, first aid kit
Food storage bags/containers, trash bags
Hand sanitizer and wipes, face masks, bar soap, dish soap, cleaning supplies
Flashlights, light bulbs, batteries, tool kit
Battery/crank radio with weather alert
Rechargeable power station for small appliances, external drives for data
Cash, traveler's checks, family documents in waterproof storage
Hobby supplies, board games, puzzles
Baby supplies, toys for kids
Shop in advance for special occasions

gān bēi

å'kålè ma'luna

à votre santé.

cin cin

BEH SALÂMATI

salud

skål

CHEERS

l'chaim prost

A New Year

The Winter Feast: Casseroles and Comfort Food

"In With the New" Black-Eyed Pea Salad

aka *Texas Caviar*

Makes 16 servings

Perfect for good luck in the New Year, or anytime! About as delicious as a salad can be. Black-eyed peas with toma-toes represent prosperity and health. Serve with cornbread, which represents gold. Bake up a quick pan of Belle Reve Honey Cornbread, page 197! In the South, cabbage or collards are frequently part of the lucky menu.

12 scallions, white and green parts, sliced thin

1 red onion, diced

1 green bell pepper, diced

1 teaspoon chili powder

½ teaspoon ground cumin

⅓ cup chopped cilantro

3 tablespoons distilled white vinegar

2 teaspoons freshly ground pepper

1 can (10 ounces) Ro-Tel tomatoes with green chilies, drained

1 can (15 ounces) whole kernel corn, drained

2 cans (15.5 ounces each) black-eyed peas, drained

In large bowl, combine scallions, red onion, green pepper, chili powder, cumin, cilantro, vinegar, black pepper, stir together thoroughly. Add Ro-Tel tomatoes, corn, black-eyed peas, stir together thoroughly. Cover and refrigerate at least 3 hours before serving.

Cream of Tomato Soup with Ham-&-Pickle Grilled Cheese Sandwiches

Soup: Makes 8 servings
Sandwich: Makes 4 servings

Pro Tip: *Dip the sandwiches in the soup as you go. A one-way ticket to paradise.*

SOUP

- 2 tablespoons butter
- 1 large shallot, minced
- 1 large clove garlic, minced
- 1 can (28 ounces) peeled tomatoes, chopped
- 1 can (6 ounces) tomato paste
- 1 quart chicken broth
- 1 teaspoon sugar
- 1 teaspoon salt
- 4 tablespoons chopped parsley, divided
- 1 heaping tablespoon prepared horseradish
- ½ cup heavy cream

In a large pot over medium-high heat melt butter. Sauté shallot and garlic till softened, 3 minutes.

Add tomatoes, tomato paste, stir to combine. Add broth, sugar, salt.

Stir thoroughly and bring mixture to a boil. Lower heat, simmer uncovered for 20 minutes, stirring occasionally. Stir in 2 tablespoons parsley and horseradish. With immersion blender (or standard blender, in batches) purée soup till smooth.

Stir in cream, garnish with remaining parsley, and serve.

SANDWICH

- ¼ cup minced kosher dill gherkins
- ¼ cup Creole or spicy coarse-grained mustard
- 8 slices round loaf whole wheat bread
- 8 slices Black Forest ham
- 8 ounces extra sharp cheddar cheese, in 16 slices
- 8 tablespoons (1 stick) butter, divided

In small bowl, combine pickle and mustard. Butter two slices of bread, each on one side. Spread pickle mixture on second side of one slice.

In large skillet over medium-high heat, melt 1 tablespoon butter. Add 1 bread slice, pickle side up. Warm 2 slices ham next to it in pan. Set ham atop mustard mixture, cover with 4 slices cheese, increase heat. Top cheese with second slice bread, butter side up. Press down, cook till cheese starts to melt and bread is golden brown. Flip, brown second side. Assemble and grill remaining sandwiches.

Spicy Split Pea Soup

Makes 12 servings

2 tablespoons butter

1 large onion, diced

4 ribs celery, diced

1 pound green split peas

5 carrots, chopped coarse

1 pound smoked ham, in ½-inch cubes

1 tablespoon dried thyme

1 bay leaf

½ teaspoon cayenne pepper

1 tablespoon salt

In large soup pot over medium-high heat melt butter, cook onion and celery till softened, about 5 minutes. Add split peas, carrots, ham, thyme, bay leaf, cayenne, salt, 8 cups water. Bring to boil, cover, leaving lid ajar, simmer till peas soften, 30 to 40 minutes. Uncover, cook till thickened, about 1 ½ hours, stirring occasionally. Let stand 20 minutes to thicken more before serving.

Pot Roast 'n Veg

Makes 8 to 10 servings

4 pounds boneless chuck roast, in four (1 pound) pieces

1 tablespoon chili powder

1 tablespoon salt

1 teaspoon freshly ground pepper

3 tablespoons olive or canola oil

2 large onions, sliced thin

2 tablespoons all-purpose flour

8 ounces white mushrooms, sliced thick

2 cups beef broth

2 tablespoons Worcestershire sauce

1 tablespoon chopped fresh rosemary

1 tablespoon fresh thyme leaves

3 large ribs celery, in 1-inch pieces

1 pound baby carrots

2 pounds small yellow potatoes

Heat oven to 350°F. Trim meat of excess fat, season on all sides with chili powder, salt, and pepper. In 7 to 8 quart Dutch oven or large oven-proof pot with tight-fitting lid, heat oil over medium-high heat. Brown meat well on all sides. Do this in two batches to avoid overcrowding. Set meat aside.

Add onions to pot, stirring to combine with brown bits. Cook onions till soft, about 5 minutes. Mix in flour till onions are coated. Add mushrooms. Arrange meat in one layer on top of onions and mushrooms. Pour beef broth and Worcestershire around meat. Sprinkle rosemary and thyme over meat. Cover pot, place in oven. After one hour, turn meat in pot, add celery, carrots, and potatoes. Baste with the liquid to moisten. Cover, return to oven. Bake for another hour, covered, till potatoes are done and meat is tender.

Blue Ribbon Chicken and Dumplings

Makes 6 servings

1 chicken (3 ½ to 4 pounds) in 8 pieces

Salt and freshly ground pepper

2 tablespoons olive oil

5 carrots, unpeeled, in ½-inch slices

5 ribs celery, in ½-inch slices

1 large onion, chopped

2 cloves garlic, minced

1 quart chicken broth

½ cup dry white wine

1 tablespoon sugar

1 tablespoon fresh thyme leaves

1 bay leaf

1 ½ cups all-purpose flour

2 teaspoons baking powder

⅔ cup buttermilk

2 tablespoons melted butter

1 cup heavy cream

1 teaspoon arrowroot starch or cornstarch

¼ cup finely chopped chives, for garnish

Season chicken lightly with salt and pepper. In Dutch oven or large pot, over medium-high heat, add oil and lightly brown chicken all over in batches, 7 to 8 minutes each, set aside. Wash any surface raw chicken has touched.

Add carrots, celery, onion, garlic, to pot. Scraping up the brown bits from chicken (aka fond, gradoux), cook vegetables till softened, 6 minutes. Add broth, wine, sugar, thyme, bay leaf. Return chicken to pot, bring liquid to boil. Reduce heat, simmer 25 minutes, partially covered, till chicken is tender. Turn chicken 2 or 3 times in pot during cooking. Discard bay leaf.

Transfer chicken to plate. When cool enough to handle, separate meat from the skin and bones. Using two forks (plus hands, but don't burn yourself!), break up meat coarsely, return to pot.

For dumplings: In a medium bowl whisk together flour, baking powder, ½ teaspoon each salt and pepper. Add buttermilk, butter. With your hands, form dumpling dough till just combined.

Return pot to simmer. Push chicken to one side of pot. Form dough into about 12 dumplings, drop in pot beside chicken. Cover and cook dumplings 15 minutes; do not stir. It's fine if they float a bit above the broth. Add heavy cream and starch, stirring gently till thickened, about 3 minutes. Serve with a generous garnish of freshly chopped chives.

Casserole Santa Fe

Makes 6 to 8 servings

A fun one to layer together. It's okay to use store-bought pre-shredded cheese in this one.

2 tablespoons canola oil

1 medium onion, chopped fine

1 cup 20-minute whole grain brown rice

2 cans (14 ½ ounces each) diced tomatoes

2 cans (4 ounces each) diced green chiles

1 ½ pounds ground beef

2 teaspoons chili powder

1 teaspoon ground cumin

2 tablespoons fresh lime juice

⅓ cup cilantro, chopped fine

1 can (15 ounces) black beans, drained

8 to 10 ounces frozen or canned corn, drained

2 cups (8 ounces) Mexican blend shredded cheese

Butter for casserole dish

Salt and freshly ground pepper

Heat oven to 350°F. Butter 9 x 13-inch baking dish.

In large heavy skillet, heat oil over medium heat. Add onions and rice and cook till onions are softened and rice is lightly toasted, 4 to 5 minutes.

Add 2 cups water, tomatoes with liquid, green chiles, lime juice, salt and pepper to taste. Simmer uncovered till rice is almost done but still has a bite to it, about 20 minutes. Transfer rice mixture to bowl and set aside.

To same skillet, add beef, chili powder, cumin, salt and pepper to taste. Cook meat just till no longer pink. Remove from heat.

In 9 x 13-inch casserole layer, in order: the black beans, half the tomato rice, the corn, the cilantro, the meat, half the cheese, remaining tomato rice, remaining cheese.

Cover with foil. Bake 45 minutes. Let sit, uncovered, 10 minutes before serving.

Shipwreck Casserole

Makes 6 to 8 servings

The "three-hour tour" casserole. With a one-two punch of rice and potatoes, it's perfect for winter weather. Historically includes celery and kidney beans; I use carrots and peas. It baked for almost two hours in days of olde (the potatoes started out raw), this one only 35 minutes. Two kinds of cheese = decidedly decadent. Grate your own good quality cheddar (I like Cracker Barrel Extra Sharp Yellow).

1 cup 20-minute whole grain brown rice, cooked al dente

1 pound ground turkey

2 tablespoons canola oil, divided

1 small sweet onion, diced

2 cloves garlic, minced

1 can (14.5 ounces) sliced potatoes, drained

1 tablespoon Creole seasoning, divided

1 can (14.5 ounces) sliced carrots

1 can (15 ounces) sweet peas

8 ounces cream cheese, in ½-inch pieces

1 can (15 ounces) tomato sauce with Italian herbs

1 cup (4 ounces) shredded sharp cheddar cheese

Salt and freshly ground pepper

Heat oven to 350°F.

Add turkey to medium skillet over medium heat, season with 1 teaspoon salt and ½ teaspoon pepper. Breaking turkey up with large spoon, cook till no longer pink. Remove from skillet and set aside.

Add 1 tablespoon oil to pan, cook onion and garlic over medium-high heat till softened, 3 minutes. Reduce heat, add cooked rice and half the Creole seasoning, stir to combine. Cook another 3 minutes, remove and set rice mixture aside.

To same pan over medium-high heat, remaining 1 tablespoon oil. Add potatoes, remaining Creole seasoning, cook till heated through, about 7 minutes.

Coat a 9 x 13-inch baking dish with cooking spray. Layer as follows: potatoes, carrots, turkey, peas. Sprinkle peas lightly with salt and pepper. Distribute chunks of cream cheese evenly over peas. Cover with the rice, then pour tomato sauce evenly over all. Top with shredded cheese. Cover with foil, bake 20 minutes. Uncover, bake 15 minutes more. Let sit 10 minutes before serving.

That's Some Kind of Tuna Casserole

Makes 4 to 6 servings

This is no traditional tuna and noodle.
One of my most popular recipes.

8 ounces fusilli or rotelle pasta

2 tablespoons olive oil

1 medium onion, diced

1 teaspoon chili powder

1 tablespoon fresh lemon juice

2 tablespoons apple cider vinegar

1 can (10.5 ounces) cream of mushroom soup

½ cup milk

3 tablespoons capers, drained

1 jar (4 ounces) diced pimentos

1 can (12 ounces) tuna in water

1 cup (4 ounces) shredded Mexican blend cheese

¼ cup (½ stick) butter

⅔ cup panko breadcrumbs

Heat oven to 350°F.

In medium pot, cook pasta two-thirds recommended time. Drain, set aside.

In large skillet, heat oil over medium-high heat. Add onion, cook till softened, about 4 minutes. Stir in chili powder, lemon juice, and cider vinegar. Add mushroom soup, milk, capers, pimentos. Stir till bubbling. Set aside.

In large bowl, use two forks to combine tuna, pasta, cheese.

Coat 8 x 8-inch (or other 2-quart) baking dish with cooking spray. Spoon half of tuna mixture into baking dish, followed by half skillet mixture, remaining tuna mixture, then rest of skillet mixture. In small pot, melt butter, add panko immediately, stir. Distribute crumbs over top of casserole. Bake uncovered 25 minutes till top is golden brown.

Rest 15 minutes. Serve to applause and fireworks.

Stairway to Heaven Mac and Cheese

Makes 6 to 8 servings

If there's a bustle in your hedgerow, don't be alarmed now. It's just a spring clean for the May queen. This mac is plenty cheesy but somehow light and heavenly too. Don't buy pre-shredded cheese, shred it yourself. This mac is best eaten right out of the oven same day. Invite friends!

3 cups (12 ounces) elbow macaroni

5 tablespoons butter, divided, more for dish

1 medium shallot, minced

2 large eggs

½ cup heavy cream

½ cup sour cream

2 cups (8 ounces) shredded sharp cheddar cheese, divided

2 cups (8 ounces) shredded pepper jack cheese

8 ounces Velveeta, in ½-inch cubes

¾ cups panko breadcrumbs

Heat oven to 350°F. Generously butter 9 x 13-inch baking dish.

Cook macaroni in salted water till al dente. In medium skillet over medium heat melt 1 tablespoon butter, cook shallot till softened and lightly colored, about 5 minutes. Let cool 5 minutes. In medium bowl, combine shallot, eggs, heavy cream, sour cream, whisk together well.

In large mixing bowl, thoroughly stir together half the cheddar, all the pepper jack, all the Velveeta, then mix in macaroni.

In baking dish, spread half macaroni mixture evenly. Pour half cream mixture evenly over that. Repeat with remaining macaroni, cover evenly with remaining cream mixture. Top with second half cheddar.

In small saucepan, melt remaining 4 tablespoons butter. Quickly stir in and fully coat panko, sprinkle mixture evenly atop casserole; you don't have to cover every inch with it.

Bake uncovered 40 minutes. Let sit 10 minutes before serving.

Game Day Snack Stadium

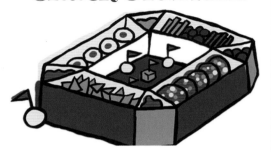

You can build one from scratch using anything from Gatorade bottles to stacked po-boy sandwiches for stadium walls, then, going inward, build in each of the stadium sections from the spectators to the field with a different kind of snack in aluminum loaf pans or box containers.

Or, buy a stadium online. Search "snack stadium" on your favorite online retail site. They range from 2 to 3 feet long and some are even inflatable. Also search "football food picks." These are festive for serving snacks, cheeses, olives.

Snacks to fill your stadium:

- Crudités: celery, carrots, grape tomatoes
- Ranch dip or my hummus for vegetables
- Po-boys or subs, sliced as single servings
- Sliced wrap sandwiches
- Hamburger sliders and taquitos
- Deviled eggs (see Patio Party chapter!)
- Pretzels, popcorn
- All your favorite crackers, and my onion dip
- Every kind of chip, Doritos, Ruffles with ridges
- Guacamole
- Salsa and chile con queso
- Rolled ham and salami on toothpicks
- Cubed and sliced cheeses: Italian & Dutch
- Pickles, olives, pepperoncini peppers
- Nuts of all kinds: peanuts, wasabi peas
- Sweets: cookies, brownies, donuts

Three Lime Chili

Makes 8 to 10 servings

A rib-sticking treat for game day. The third lime's a charm! Great with Belle Reve Honey Cornbread from my Thanksgiving chapter.

2 tablespoons olive oil, divided

4 cloves garlic, minced, divided

2 pounds ground sirloin, or other lean ground beef

1 ½ pounds ground turkey

1 large sweet onion, diced

2 bell peppers, yellow and/or orange, diced

1 can (4 ounces) diced green chiles

2 tablespoons chili powder

1 tablespoon ground cumin

1 can (28 ounces) crushed tomatoes

1 can (15.5 ounces) pink beans

Juice of 3 limes

Salt and freshly ground pepper

In a large Dutch oven or heavy pot over medium-high heat, heat 1 tablespoon oil and half the minced garlic. Cook beef and turkey till no longer pink. Season with salt and pepper as desired. Drain fat, set meat aside. Add remaining 1 tablespoon oil, garlic, onion, cook till softened, 4 minutes. Add bell pepper, green chiles, chili powder, cumin, tomatoes. Stir till mixture starts to simmer. Add beef and turkey, mix well.

Reduce heat to low, cook covered for 1 ½ hours, stirring every 10 to 15 minutes. Mix in pink beans and lime juice. Simmer on low 30 minutes more, stirring frequently. Serve immediately, or the next day, giving flavors time to meld overnight. Serve over rice. Top with chopped scallions and/or shredded cheese. Serve with cornbread or corn muffins.

Cooking Tips & Tricks

How to avoid a Hail Mary

1. Taste as you cook. You might have put salt in, instead of sugar. You don't know, if you don't taste!

2. Follow baking recipes without variation. If you make impulsive changes, you may experience ignominious failure.

3. Don't overcrowd the pan when browning or frying. Leave the food alone till it's time to turn it.

4. Start cooking early so you don't have to rush. Plan ahead. Write your menu out, study your recipes, organize your ingredients. Things like a vegetable trinity (chopped onion, celery, bell pepper) can be made a day or two in advance and refrigerated in plastic bags.

5. How to cut a bell pepper for strips or dicing: Hold pepper stem side down and cut off each lobe individually with a downward slicing motion, taking care not to encounter the seeds in the center of the pepper as you slice. You will have 3 to 4 full sections of pepper and the stem and core can be quickly discarded as one tidy piece. Then proceed to make strips or dice.

6. Onions make you cry? Put 'em in the freezer for 20 to 30 minutes before cutting. They might chill your fingers but you won't need your tissues!

7. To keep brown sugar from becoming rock hard once opened, fill extra space in the bag with marshmallows and tightly close.

8. Before measuring peanut butter, honey, and molasses, spray the spoon with cooking spray. Tacky ingredients slide out easy and cleanup's a breeze.

9. The shells of boiled eggs come off more easily if you add a tablespoon of vinegar to the water when simmering. Older eggs also peel more easily than fresh eggs.

10. When a recipe says to use an ingredient at room temperature, do it! Room temperature butter, eggs, and meat, make for much more beautifully textured, juicy, fluffy, tender results. What to do? Let an ingredient sit out for 45 to 60 minutes before using.

Cookies of Many Lands

Champion Chocolate Chip Chubbies

USA

Makes 40 cookies. DOUGH MUST BE REFRIGERATED OVERNIGHT.
Follow the recipe to the letter for best results.

2 ½ cups unbleached all-purpose flour

2 teaspoons arrowroot starch or cornstarch

1 teaspoon baking powder

1 teaspoon baking soda

1 cup (2 sticks) unsalted butter, softened

½ teaspoon salt

1 ¼ cups packed light brown sugar

½ cup granulated sugar

2 large eggs

1 tablespoon vanilla extract

2 cups semisweet chocolate chips (12-ounce bag)

In medium bowl, whisk together flour, starch, baking powder, baking soda. In large bowl, using electric mixer, cream butter, salt, and both sugars till fluffy, about 3 minutes. Add eggs one at a time, mixing till just incorporated. Mix in vanilla. Add flour mixture in two batches, don't over mix. With wooden spoon, stir in chocolate chips till evenly distributed. Cover dough tightly or wrap in plastic and refrigerate overnight. Don't skip this step.

Heat oven to 350°F. Line two baking sheets with parchment paper. Working with hard, still-chilled dough, place hand-rolled 1 ¼-inch diameter balls of dough 1 ½ inches apart on prepared cookie sheets. Bake two sheets of cookies at a time. Refrigerate dough between batches. Bake for 9 to 11 minutes and watch closely! Pull cookies out when they have a hint of gold. Transfer carefully to cooling racks, or cool on the sheets if they seem too soft. They will firm up as they cool.

Best if cooled for at least 20 minutes before serving. (Or scarf 'em down right away, I won't judge.) Store tightly covered in a cool place.

Nanaimo Bars *CANADA*

Makes 24 bars

10 ounces semisweet chocolate chips, divided

1 cup (2 sticks), and 2 tablespoons softened butter, divided

1 large egg, beaten

2 cups graham cracker crumbs

1 cup flaked sweetened coconut

½ cup chopped walnuts

3 tablespoons heavy cream

2 tablespoons arrowroot starch or corn starch

2 cups confectioners' sugar

Heat oven to 350°F. Melt 2 ounces (⅓ cup) chocolate chips in microwave, watching carefully. In medium bowl, stir together 1 stick butter and the melted chips. Add beaten egg. Add cracker crumbs, coconut, walnuts. Press mixture evenly into ungreased 8 x 8-inch baking dish. Bake for 8 minutes, cool. In medium bowl, whisk together 1 stick butter, heavy cream, and starch till velvety. Add confectioners' sugar and combine well. Spread mixture over graham cracker layer, refrigerate 30 minutes. Melt 8 ounces (1 ⅓ cups) chocolate chips with remaining 2 tablespoons butter in microwave, or on stove over low heat. Spread melted chocolate over sugar as top layer. Refrigerate 1 hour, then cut into 24 bars. Refrigerate between servings.

Strawberry-Chocolate Alfajores *ARGENTINA*

Makes 16 sandwich cookies

3 cups unbleached all-purpose flour

½ cup sugar

½ teaspoon baking powder

1 teaspoon salt

1 cup (2 sticks) butter softened

¼ cup canola oil

1 cup organic strawberry preserves

8 ounces semisweet chocolate chips (1 ⅓ cups)

8 ounces flaked sweetened coconut

Heat oven to 350°F. Grease 2 cookie sheets. In large bowl, whisk together flour, sugar, baking powder, salt. Add butter and oil. Using hands, make dough. On floured surface, roll out dough ⅛-inch thick. Using 2-inch round cookie cutter, cut 32 cookies and place on greased sheets ½-inch apart. Bake 15 minutes till slightly golden around edges. Cool on baking sheets.

Coat medium heatproof bowl with cooking spray. Add chocolate chips and set bowl over small pot with 2 inches of simmering water. Make sure water doesn't touch bowl. When chocolate is melted, move quickly through next steps. Using a tablespoon, spread chocolate on 16 of the cookies. Then spread a teaspoon of preserves over chocolate. Sprinkle each generously with coconut. To finish, spread one tablespoon of chocolate on each of the remaining 16 cookies then sandwich with the first 16 halves. Refrigerate for one hour so chocolate hardens. Cover and keep chilled between servings.

Spritz Cookies (Spritzgebäck)

GERMANY

Makes about 6 dozen cookies

Special equipment: cookie press. I use the Preferred Press from Wilton. These are double-thick, you push press twice.

3 ½ cups unbleached all-purpose flour

2 teaspoons baking powder

1 teaspoon arrowroot starch or cornstarch

1 teaspoon salt

1 ½ cups (3 sticks) unsalted butter, softened

1 cup sugar

1 large egg

2 tablespoons milk

1 teaspoon vanilla

One or more colors sanding sugar appropriate for the occasion

Heat oven to 350°F.

In a medium bowl, whisk together flour, baking powder, starch, salt. In a large bowl, with electric mixer, cream together butter and sugar till fluffy, about 2 minutes. Mix in one whole egg, then mix in milk, vanilla. With hands, mix in dry ingredients in two additions till smooth dough forms.

Using cookie press, place cookies 1 inch apart on ungreased cookie sheets. Click twice per cookie for thicker results. Sprinkle with sanding sugar as desired.

Bake 8 to 10 minutes on center rack till edges are just lightly colored. The bottoms should be light brown. Don't over bake.

Cool on wire racks.

Cinnamon Tahini Cookies *ISRAEL*

Makes 24 cookies

3 cups unbleached all-purpose flour

1 cup sugar

2 teaspoons baking powder

1 tablespoon ground cinnamon

1 cup (2 sticks) unsalted butter, melted

1 cup tahini (stir in any separated oil before measuring)

5 ounces toasted sesame seeds

Heat oven to 350°F. Grease two cookie sheets. In large bowl, whisk together flour, sugar, baking powder, cinnamon. With hands or large wooden spoon, mix in butter and tahini till dough forms.

Roll dough into 1 ½-inch balls, then coat with sesame seeds. Place on prepared cookie sheets, flattening balls slightly. These cookies do not spread so you can place them close to each other. Bake for 20 to 25 minutes till lightly colored. Transfer to wire rack and cool at least 30 minutes. They should be soft and crumbly inside.

Persian Walnut Cookies (Naan Gerdooee)

Makes 24 cookies

6 egg yolks (reserving 2 whites)

½ cup confectioners' sugar

½ teaspoon vanilla extract

1 teaspoon baking soda

1 teaspoon ground cardamom

½ teaspoon ground cinnamon

¼ teaspoon ground nutmeg

3 cups very finely chopped walnuts
   (about 12 ounces whole walnuts)

24 walnut halves for decoration

Heat oven to 300°F. Grease two cookie sheets.

In large bowl, with electric mixer, beat yolks. Add sugar and beat till mixture becomes pale, about 5 minutes. Add vanilla, baking soda, cardamom, cinnamon, nutmeg, chopped walnuts, and using wooden spoon combine thoroughly.

Using a small cookie scoop or teaspoon drop 1-inch balls onto cookie sheets and top each with one walnut half. These cookies do not spread. Brush the top of each cookie with lightly beaten egg white. Bake for about 25 minutes till cookies are lightly colored. Cool on wire racks.

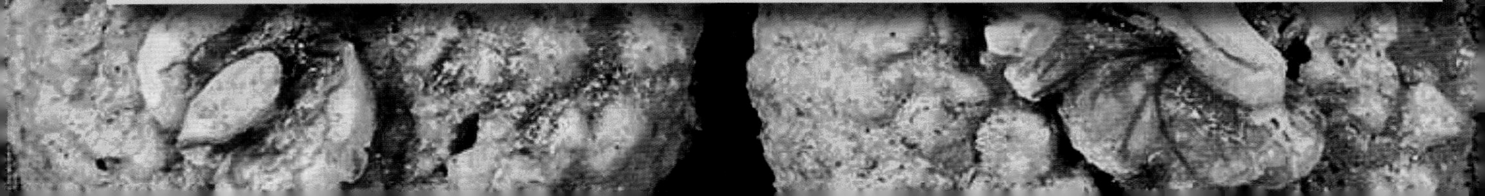

Maids of Honour *ENGLAND*

Makes 24 tartlets

The tarts that inspire this recipe are quite historic in Britain however nobody I know in London has ever heard of them! They're from the time of King Henry VIII, and, of course, all my friends are much younger. This is one of my very favorite recipes. Hashtag: sinful. You be the judge.

1 ½ cups unbleached all-purpose flour

1 teaspoon baking powder

1 teaspoon salt

½ cup (1 stick) salted butter, softened

½ cup sugar

2 tablespoons whole milk

½ teaspoon white distilled vinegar

8 ounces 100% fruit red raspberry preserves

6 tablespoons (¾ stick) salted butter, softened

3 tablespoons sugar

1 egg white, lightly beaten

1 cup walnuts, chopped very fine

½ teaspoon almond extract

Heat oven to 350°F. Generously spray a 24-cup mini muffin pan with cooking spray. Do this inside your open dishwasher for easy cleanup.

For bottom crust: In small bowl, whisk together flour, baking powder, salt. In medium bowl, using electric mixer, cream 1 stick butter and ½ cup sugar till fluffy. Add milk and vinegar, stir well. Add dry ingredients, use hands to form dough. If crumbly, give it a good squoosh. Divide in halves. Divide each half into 12 pieces, fill the cups. Press finger down hard in the center to make a nook for preserves. Dough should press up the sides of each cup to just below the edge. Bake for 9 to 10 minutes till set but not browned.

For topping: In medium bowl, stir 5 tablespoons butter, 3 tablespoons sugar, egg white, walnuts, almond extract. Fill each crust with a half teaspoon preserves. Divide topping evenly among tartlets, covering and sealing in filling. Bake for 18 to 20 minutes. Cool for 10 minutes in pan. Help each out with a knife. You might have a few imperfections. The more rustic they look, the better they taste.

Sweet Satay Peanut Crumbles *INDONESIA*

Makes 54 cookies

Sweet Satay Peanut Crumbles are the "cookie incarnation" of the Indonesian peanut dipping sauce that accompanies their national dish, the satay skewer. This uncommonly moist, crumbly creation takes the cookie-friendly elements of the satay flavor profile to a new, addictive level.

1 cup smooth low sodium and sugar creamy peanut butter

1 cup (2 sticks) salted butter, softened

1 cup brown sugar

½ cup white sugar

3 large eggs

2 tablespoons coconut extract

¼ cup fresh lime juice

¼ cup honey

¼ cup soy sauce

3 tablespoons tomato ketchup

2 ½ cups unbleached all-purpose flour

1 teaspoon baking powder

1 teaspoon ground cinnamon

1 teaspoon ground nutmeg

1 teaspoon salt

6 ounces salted peanuts, for topping

Heat oven to 375°F. Spray two cookie sheets with cooking spray.

In large bowl, using electric hand mixer, cream together peanut butter, butter, both sugars. Incorporate eggs, one at a time, mix in coconut extract, lime juice, honey, soy sauce, ketchup. Stir till smooth. In another bowl, whisk together flour, baking powder, cinnamon, nutmeg, salt. Gradually add dry ingredients to wet, stirring with wooden spoon till just combined. Using a 2 tablespoon scoop for each cookie, drop dough on prepared cookie sheets, leaving 1 inch between cookies. Top each cookie with 4 to 5 peanuts, pushing in lightly.

Bake for 15 to 17 minutes, till outer edges show slight browning. Remove to racks to cool. Interiors should be quite moist. It's ok if a peanut or two falls off or they come apart as you eat them. That's the way *this* cookie crumbles!!

Chinese Restaurant Almond Cookies

Makes 30 cookies

2 ½ cups unbleached all-purpose flour

1 cup sugar

1 teaspoon baking powder

1 teaspoon salt

1 cup lard or shortening, room temperature, in ½-inch pieces

1 large egg

1 teaspoon almond extract

30 whole toasted almonds

1 egg white and 1 teaspoon water whisked together

Heat oven to 350°F.

In large bowl, whisk together flour, sugar, baking powder, salt. Add lard, egg, almond extract, to dry ingredients. With hands, work mixture till dough forms.

On two ungreased cookie sheets, place 1-inch balls of dough 2 inches apart. Press an almond into top of each, flattening each ball slightly. Brush tops of cookies with egg white and water glaze. Bake 12 to 15 minutes till slightly browned. Cool on wire racks.

On the Occasion of the Chinese New Year

Hot-and-Sour Soup

Makes 4 Servings

Let's start this year off with a bang! This is probably my favorite Chinese dish. Popular in Beijing, Shanghai, and Chengdu, it often includes dried lilies, tree ear fungus, and pig blood. I'm telling you this to make you feel better about the tofu. Also very satisfying as a main.

⅓ cup soy sauce	1 can (8 ounces) sliced bamboo shoots, drained, cut in strips
⅓ cup distilled white vinegar	1 large carrot, cut in thin strips, about 1 ½ cups
½ teaspoon sugar	2 teaspoons grated fresh ginger
1 teaspoon ground white pepper	1 large egg, well beaten
3 tablespoons cornstarch	7 ounces firm tofu, cut in ½-inch cubes
4 cups chicken broth	3 large scallions, green parts only, sliced on the diagonal
8 ounces fresh shiitake mushrooms, stemmed, cut in strips	2 teaspoons toasted sesame oil

In medium bowl, whisk together soy sauce, vinegar, sugar, pepper, cornstarch.

In large pot bring broth and two cups water to boil. Add mushrooms, bamboo shoots, carrot, ginger, return to boil. Reduce heat and simmer, covered, till mushrooms and carrots are tender, 6 to 8 minutes. Stir cornstarch mixture briefly to recombine, add to pot while stirring, return to simmer, do not boil.

Stirring soup in a circular motion, drizzle in the egg and watch as ribbons form. Add tofu, half the scallions, sesame oil. Stir gently to combine.

When tofu is heated through, about 3 minutes, you are ready to serve. Garnish with remaining sliced scallions.

Sichuan Peanut Noodles

Makes 6 side servings

Red chili and coriander are similar in flavor to sichuan peppercorns. If you have the real thing, even better. These noodles are rustic-textured and sublime.

½ pound bucatini, fettuccine, linguini

⅓ cup natural peanut butter

3 tablespoons soy sauce

2 tablespoons peanut oil

1 tablespoon distilled white vinegar

1 teaspoon toasted sesame oil

1 tablespoon sugar

1 teaspoon ground coriander

½ teaspoon red chili flakes

Juice of 2 limes

Break pasta in half and cook according to package directions, drain, set aside. When pasta pot has cooled, dry thoroughly and in it combine peanut butter, peanut oil, soy sauce, vinegar, sesame oil, sugar, coriander, chili flakes. Over medium heat, stir mixture till well blended. Cook till you get just a hint of a simmer. Pull off heat and immediately fold in noodles, add lime juice. Stir vigorously. Chill, covered, 30 minutes, serve cold.

Baby Bok Choy

Makes 4 servings

9 baby bok choy clusters about 6 inches each

2 tablespoons soy sauce

2 tablespoons distilled white vinegar

1 teaspoon toasted sesame oil

½ teaspoon sugar

½ teaspoon ground white pepper

2 tablespoons canola oil

6 slices peeled ginger

2 cloves garlic, sliced

¼ cup water

Remove any limp outer leaves, trim bases of clusters. Wash out dirt at base of leaves, pat dry. Cut each cluster in half lengthwise.

In small bowl, whisk together soy sauce, vinegar, sesame oil, sugar, pepper.

In large skillet or wok, heat canola oil over high heat. Add ginger and garlic, stir-fry till fragrant, about half a minute. Add bok choy, cook, stirring, one minute. Add soy sauce mixture. Stir briskly for another minute till bok choy is glazed with soy sauce mixture. Add water, stir, reduce heat to low, cover for 4 minutes to steam. Serve while hot, with sauce from the skillet.

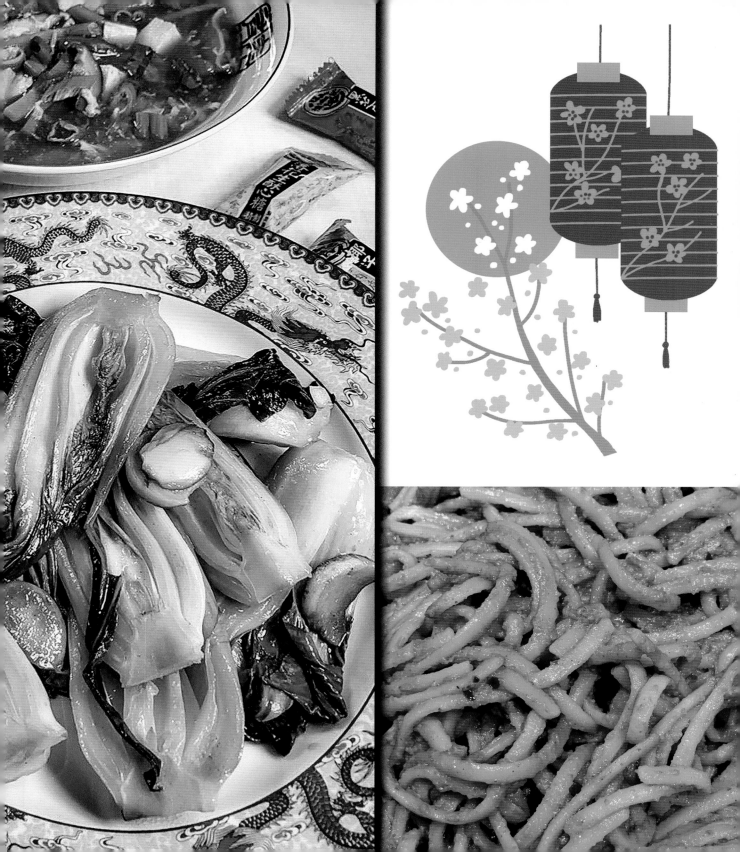

Fisherman's Chop Suey

Makes 4 servings

Living here is very much like chop suey.
— *Oscar Hammerstein II*

¼ cup canola oil

1 pound white fish: cod or haddock, cut in 1-inch chunks

1 cup carrots, cut diagonally in ½-inch slices

1 cup celery, cut diagonally in ½-inch slices

1 cup red bell pepper, cut in 1-inch triangles

1 can (14 ounces) baby corn, whole or pieces, drained
    and patted dry

2 tablespoons cornstarch

2 tablespoons soy sauce

2 tablespoons sherry

½ teaspoon sugar

1 teaspoon salt, divided

½ teaspoon freshly ground pepper

1 cup vegetable broth

¼ to ½ teaspoon red chili flakes

¾ pound medium to large shrimp, tails off

1 cup scallions, white and green parts, cut diagonally in
    ½-inch slices

2 teaspoons toasted sesame oil

In small bowl, whisk arrowroot, soy sauce, and ¼ cup water together and set aside.

In second small bowl, combine sherry, sugar, ½ teaspoon salt, black pepper.

In large deep skillet or wok over medium-high heat add oil and heat till shimmers. Standing back in case of spattering, add sherry mixture and fish to pan. Stir-fry till fish is opaque, 2 to 3 minutes. Transfer fish to a bowl and set aside.

To skillet, add carrots, celery, bell pepper, corn, and stir-fry to coat with pan liquid. Add broth and red pepper flakes. Bring liquid to boil, reduce heat and simmer till vegetables are crisp-tender, stirring, about 10 minutes.

Add shrimp and remaining ½ teaspoon salt. Stir-fry till shrimp turn pink, about 5 minutes. Return fish to skillet, add scallions. Add soy sauce mixture, continue cooking till sauce thickens, 3 to 4 minutes. Serve over hot rice, drizzled with sesame oil and garnished with scallions.

Shanghai Fried Rice

Makes 4 to 6 servings

The venerated and delectable Chinese staple.

    3 cups cooked jasmine rice, frozen per below
    ¼ cup soy sauce
    1 teaspoon salt
    1 teaspoon sugar
    1 teaspoon white pepper
    1 tablespoon toasted sesame oil
    3 tablespoons canola oil, divided
    2 eggs, lightly beaten
    1 tablespoon minced garlic
    1 tablespoon minced ginger
    ¾ cup fresh carrot, small dice
    ½ pound ham, cut in ½" cubes
    1 cup frozen green peas
    4 large scallions, white and green parts, cut
        diagonally, divided

For frozen rice: Spread cooked rice on cookie sheet
in thin layer, freeze uncovered, for about an hour.
In a small bowl, whisk together soy sauce, sugar, salt, pepper, sesame oil. Break frozen rice into
large chunks. In a large skillet or wok, heat 1 tablespoon canola oil over medium-high heat. Add eggs,
scramble softly, about one minute, set aside. Add
remaining canola oil. When oil is almost smoking,
add garlic, ginger, stir-fry till fragrant, 30 seconds.
Add carrots and ham, stir-fry 2 minutes. Add rice,
peas, ⅔ scallions, stir-fry, breaking rice up, till
well combined. Add soy sauce mixture, stir-fry
till rice is fully coated. Add scrambled egg, stir till
heated. Garnish with remaining scallions.

50

Kung Pao Shrimp and Broccoli

Makes 4 servings

- 3 tablespoons mirin or rice wine
- 2 tablespoons arrowroot starch or cornstarch
- 2 tablespoons toasted sesame oil
- 28 large peeled shrimp, deveined, tails removed
- 1 tablespoon peanut oil
- ⅓ cup cashews
- Whole dried red chili peppers, about 12, seeded to reduce heat if desired
- 1 teaspoon minced garlic
- 1 teaspoon minced fresh ginger
- 1 package (10 ounces) frozen broccoli florets
- 1 green bell pepper, chopped
- 3 scallions, white and green parts, sliced
- ¼ cup soy sauce
- ¼ cup rice vinegar, divided
- 1 tablespoon sugar

In medium bowl, whisk together rice wine, starch, sesame oil. Add shrimp and marinate 20 minutes in fridge. In large skillet or wok, heat peanut oil over medium heat. Add cashews and chili peppers, stir-fry till fragrant, about 2 minutes. Add garlic and ginger, cook 1 minute. Add broccoli, green pepper, half the scallions, stir-fry 2 minutes more. Add soy sauce, 2 tablespoons rice vinegar, sugar, ¼ cup water. Increase heat to medium-high and bring to simmer. Add shrimp with marinade, cook till shrimp are just pink. Splash with remaining 2 tablespoons rice vinegar, transfer to serving dish and sprinkle with scallions.

Paradise Almond Chicken

Makes 4 servings

The Italian green beans in this one are quite cordial, if unorthodox. Recipe moves fast, be prepared.

- ¼ cup mirin or rice wine
- ¼ cup soy sauce
- 1 tablespoon sugar
- 1 teaspoon anise seed
- 2 tablespoons toasted sesame oil
- 2 tablespoons peanut oil, divided
- ¾ cup (about 3 ounces) raw sliced almonds
- 1 teaspoon minced garlic
- 1 tablespoon grated fresh ginger
- 1 pound boneless chicken breast, sliced thin
- 1 can (14.5 ounces) Italian green beans, drained
- 4 scallions, white and green parts, sliced thin

For sauce: in bowl, whisk together rice wine, soy sauce, sugar, star anise, sesame oil.

In a large skillet over medium-high heat, add 1 tablespoon peanut oil. Toast almonds quickly till just a bit browned, 2 to 3 minutes, set aside.

To skillet, add remaining tablespoon peanut oil over medium-high heat. Stir-fry garlic and ginger till fragrant, 30 seconds, add chicken, cook till no longer pink. Reduce heat, add sauce mixture.

Simmer till chicken is done, about 7 minutes. Add almonds, green beans, and scallions, cook till heated through, about 3 minutes. Serve over rice.

Sweet and Pungent Pork with Snow Peas

Makes 6 servings

Adapted from The House of Chan Cookbook, *1952.*

2 eggs, lightly beaten

½ cup flour

1 teaspoon each salt and freshly ground pepper

1 ¼ pounds boneless loin pork chops, cut in ¾-inch cubes

5 tablespoons peanut oil, divided

1 green bell pepper, coarsely chopped

6 ounces fresh snow peas

1 can (14.5 ounces) diced tomatoes, drained

1 can (8 ounces) crushed pineapple, drained

¼ cup rice vinegar

¼ cup distilled white vinegar

3 tablespoons brown sugar

2 tablespoons arrowroot starch or cornstarch

For dredging: make two plates with egg in first, flour plus salt and pepper in second. In large skillet or wok, heat 4 tablespoons oil over medium-high till shimmering. Working quickly, dredge pork in egg then flour and add to pan. Stir-fry, cooking pork till no longer pink, about 5 minutes. Set meat aside.

To skillet, add 1 tablespoon oil, stir-fry green pepper and snow peas, about 2 minutes. Add tomatoes and pineapple, cook another 2 minutes to heat.

Add rice and white vinegars, brown sugar, starch. Return pork to pan and cook over medium heat to incorporate flavors, about 5 minutes. Serve over rice.

Spicy Pepper Beef *Makes 4 servings*

1 ¼ pounds sirloin steak, cut across grain into ¼-inch slices

2 tablespoons distilled white vinegar

⅓ cup soy sauce

1 tablespoon brown sugar

1 tablespoon peeled, grated fresh ginger

1 teaspoon white pepper

2 teaspoons arrowroot starch or cornstarch

3 tablespoons canola oil

3 cloves garlic, sliced thin

1 large red bell pepper, sliced thin

1 large green bell pepper, sliced thin

5 scallions, white and green parts, cut on a diagonal, divided

1 ½ teaspoons toasted sesame oil

For easier slicing, put steak in freezer till partially frozen, about an hour. In medium bowl, whisk together vinegar, soy sauce, sugar, ginger, white pepper. Marinate steak 30 minutes. Remove beef, pat dry, set aside. Reserve marinade, add starch, stir, set aside. In a large skillet or wok, heat canola oil till shimmering, almost smoking. Stir-fry beef, in batches, so browned on outside but still pink inside, about 2 minutes per batch. Set aside. Reduce heat, add garlic, stir-fry till fragrant, about 30 seconds. Add bell peppers and soften, about 2 minutes. Stir marinade mixture to recombine. Return beef to pan, add marinade mixture, stir-fry 2 minutes. Add ⅔ scallions, stir-fry another 2 minutes. Finish with toasted sesame oil. Serve with rice, garnish with remaining scallions.

A Valentine in Paris

Salade de Lentilles
(Lentil Salad)

Makes 8 to 10 servings

If French food is the grand opera of cuisines, Paris is its opera house. One of the most rhapsodic restaurants in town, Chez Georges, excels at a popular French dish: a delicious vinaigrette salad with French lentilles du Puy, Puy being the region that grows them. Of course in France, as in Italy, many foods come from a region with its own specialty.

1 pound French lentils, or green lentils, picked over

4 cups chicken broth

5 sprigs fresh thyme

1 bay leaf

⅓ cup olive oil plus one tablespoon, divided

1 large red onion, diced

2 cloves garlic, minced

1 tablespoon coarse-grain mustard

2 tablespoons apple cider vinegar

½ cup chopped parsley

Coarsely ground fresh pepper

In Dutch oven or large pot cover lentils with broth plus water to cover by one inch, add thyme, bay leaf.

Bring to boil, simmer till lentils are almost done but still have a firmness, 20 to 30 minutes. Remove bay leaf, thyme, drain.

In small skillet heat 1 tablespoon oil over medium-high, add onion, garlic, cook till softened, about 5 minutes.

For dressing, in large bowl, briskly whisk together mustard, vinegar, ⅓ cup oil.

Add onion mixture to dressing and spoon over hot lentils. Stir thoroughly. Add parsley, 3 or 4 grinds coarse ground pepper, give it another light stir. Serve while still warm, or slightly chilled.

Soupe à l'oignon

Makes 6 servings

4 tablespoons (½ stick) butter

4 large yellow onions, about 2 ½ pounds, sliced thin

½ teaspoon salt

½ teaspoon freshly ground pepper

1 teaspoon brown sugar

2 cloves garlic, chopped

⅓ cup port wine

2 tablespoons all-purpose flour

7 cups beef broth

French baguette, cut in 1" cubes

3 cups (9 ounces) Gruyère cheese, shredded

2 tablespoons minced parsley

In a large Dutch oven or heavy soup pot over medium heat melt butter, add onions. Cook 8 to 10 minutes stirring occasionally till softened. Increase heat to medium-high, add sugar, salt, pepper, cook onions till caramelized, stirring frequently, 30 minutes. Stir in garlic, cook 5 minutes. Add port, cook 5 to 7 minutes. Add flour, stir till mixture thickens, about 2 minutes. Gradually add broth, simmer, stirring occasionally, 20 to 25 minutes till flavor satisfies.

Heat oven to 350°F. On a sheet pan bake baguette cubes till browned, about 7 minutes.

Fill six oven-proof bowls with 3 or 4 baguette cubes then fill each with soup. Top each bowl with ½ cup cheese from edge to edge. Turn on broiler and place bowls on sheet pan. Carefully place sheet pan on center oven rack for more control. Melt cheese till lightly browned. Serve with a garnish of parsley.

Camembert Cœurs d'Amour

Makes 2 servings

Because it's Valentine's! In Europe, one can buy Brie and Neufchâtel in heart shapes. In the USA we need to be creative.

1 (8 ounce) wheel of Camembert cheese

½ cup dried cranberries

⅓ cup dried apricots

½ cup dried Turkish figs

⅓ cup toasted whole almonds

Sprigs of parsley

1 baguette, sliced

Make 2 of these plates, one for each Valentine, or just 1 for both to share. The following is for 2. Cut the wheel of Camembert in quarters, cut a triangle out of the curved edge of each wedge to make a heart. (See photo). Place wedges with bottom points of the hearts facing each other. Surround with cranberries, figs, apricots, almonds, and a couple of sprigs of parsley. Serve with a sliced baguette and your favorite French wine.

Pâté de Campagne (Country Pâté)

Makes 8 servings

You never thought you'd make a French country pâté from scratch, now did you? Well now's your chance! It's fun to do and it's just like the real McCoy.

1 tablespoon butter	2 tablespoons flour
1 medium shallot, chopped fine	1 large egg
2 cloves garlic, minced	1 tablespoon salt
1 ½ pounds ground pork	1 teaspoon coarsely ground fresh pepper
8-ounce ham steak, in ½-inch cubes	1 teaspoon dried thyme
6 ounces chicken livers, deveined, chopped fine	½ teaspoon ground allspice
½ red bell pepper, ¼-inch dice	½ teaspoon cayenne pepper
¼ cup cornichons or kosher dills, diced	⅓ cup Cognac
⅓ cup heavy cream	12 slices bacon for lining pan

In small skillet melt butter, cook shallot and garlic till softened, about 4 minutes. In a large bowl combine ground pork, ham, chicken liver, bell pepper, cornichons. In a small bowl whisk together cream, flour, egg, salt, pepper, thyme, allspice, cayenne. Add softened shallot, cream mixture, and cognac to bowl with meat mixture. Use fork to combine well.

Heat oven to 350°F.

Line a 8 ½ x 4 ½ x 3-inch loaf pan with strips of bacon. Overlap the strips so there are no gaps, letting the ends hang over the edge. Add strips on the ends so pâté will be fully covered. Gently spoon in meat mixture, then pack firmly. Drop pan onto counter several times, to eliminate air pockets. The filling, once covered with bacon, should be at a level just below rim of pan. If necessary, cover any gaps with additional bacon so pâté is fully enclosed. Cut a piece of parchment paper the size of the top of the pan, place over bacon. Cover top of pan tightly with foil, making a tight seal.

On center rack of oven, place large pan with high sides. Set pâté loaf pan in center of the large pan. Carefully fill large pan with hot water halfway up the sides of the loaf pan.

Bake 1 ½ to 2 hours till a thermometer in thickest part of pâté reads at least 165°F. Remove pâté from oven. Rest for 15 minutes then refrigerate, still covered, for 6 hours or overnight. To turn pâté out of loaf pan, rest pan in warm water for about a minute, uncover, then invert pâté onto a large flat plate. You can easily clean off any jellied fat that has separated during chilling.

Serve sliced, with additional (whole) cornichons, a zesty French mustard, a handful of sliced radishes and a good crusty baguette.

Coq au Champagne *Makes 4 servings*

Coq au vin, with bubbles.

- 4 large chicken breasts, skin-on, bone-in
- 4 tablespoons butter, divided
- 8 ounces sliced white mushrooms
- 2 medium carrots in ½-inch slices
- 2 ribs celery in ½-inch slices
- 1 shallot, chopped fine
- 2 cloves garlic, minced
- 3 tablespoons flour
- 2 cups of a nice French champagne (Never point cork towards your head! Share the rest with friends as you cook.)
- 1 cup chicken broth
- 2 tablespoons fresh tarragon, minced
- 4 sprigs fresh thyme
- 1 bay leaf
- Salt and freshly ground pepper

Heat oven to 350°F. Liberally salt and pepper chicken on all sides. In a Dutch oven or large heavy pot over medium-high heat, melt 2 tablespoons butter. Cook chicken and brown lightly on all sides, about 10 minutes. Set chicken aside. Reduce heat to medium, add remaining 2 tablespoons butter. Add mushrooms, stirring occasionally till golden brown, about 8 minutes. Add the carrots, celery, shallot, and garlic, cook till shallot has softened. To "singer" (sawn-ZHAY) the vegetables (that's French for combining flour with ingredients cooked in fat), mix in flour and stir lightly.

Add champagne and deglaze bottom of the pot, scraping up the tasty brown bits as you stir in the bubbly.

Bring to simmer then add broth, tarragon, thyme, bay leaf, stirring briskly to help fully cook in the flour. Now submerge the chicken in its lovely bath of champagne and vegetables. Cover pot and cook in oven till chicken is done to perfection, 40 to 50 minutes. Remove thyme sprigs, and bay leaf.

Ratatouille Rive Droite *Makes 6 to 8 servings*

- 6 tablespoons olive oil, divided
- 1 yellow onion, sliced in thin crescents
- 2 cloves garlic, chopped
- 1 ½ teaspoons salt, divided
- 1 eggplant (about 1 pound), in ½-inch cubes
- 2 medium zucchini squash, in ¼-inch slices
- 1 medium yellow squash, cut in thin half moons
- 10 ounces grape tomatoes
- 4 sprigs fresh thyme
- ⅓ cup chopped flat-leaf parsley
- 1 teaspoon dried oregano
- 1 bay leaf
- ⅓ cup white wine
- 6 basil leaves, cut in chiffonade

In large skillet, heat two tablespoons oil over medium-high. Add onion, garlic, ½ teaspoon salt, cook till softened, 4 minutes. Transfer pan contents to Dutch oven. Add another 2 tablespoons oil to skillet, add eggplant and 1 teaspoon salt, cook till lightly colored, 6 to 8 minutes. To Dutch oven, add eggplant as next layer, without stirring. To the skillet add another 2 tablespoons oil, cook both squashes till yellow squash is translucent, about 5 minutes. Transfer to Dutch oven as next layer.

To Dutch oven, without stirring, add tomatoes, thyme, parsley, oregano, bay leaf, wine.

Simmer gently, covered, till tomatoes have wilted and vegetables are tender, about 20 minutes. Do not overcook. Now you may stir it all together, garnish with basil chiffonade, and serve!

Poulet Rôti Saint-Germain

Aromatic Roast Chicken

Makes 4 to 6 servings

3 to 4 pound whole chicken

2 teaspoons salt, divided

1 tablespoon fresh thyme leaves, plus 4 whole sprigs

4 sprigs fresh tarragon

8 sprigs parsley, divided

2 bay leaves

1 lemon, halved

1 head of garlic, halved crosswise

1 shallot, halved lengthwise

3 strips thick bacon

½ cup (1 stick) salted butter, melted

Freshly ground pepper

An hour before you begin, pat the chicken dry with paper towels, rub all over inside and out with 1 teaspoon salt. Refrigerate. Wash your hands thoroughly.

Heat oven to 450°F.

Stuff cavity of chicken with 4 sprigs each of thyme, tarragon, and parsley, and the bay leaves. Insert lemon half, garlic half, shallot half. Tie legs together with kitchen twine. After handling raw chicken remember to wash hands, as well as all in-contact kitchen equipment.

In a large Dutch oven cook the bacon on stovetop till softened, about 5 minutes.

Place the bird breast up in pan, arrange partially cooked bacon around it. Then surround with remaining halves of garlic, lemon, shallot, and rest of parsley.

Pour melted butter over entire bird. Sprinkle with remaining teaspoon salt and shower with several generous grinds of pepper. Finish with the tablespoon of thyme leaves, evenly scattered.

Roast chicken for 45-55 minutes and test with thermometer in thickest part of the breast. When it makes it to 165°F you're done.

Sole Meunière Amandine

Makes 4 Servings

- Four (6 ounce) fillets of sole or any lean fish like flounder, snapper, cod
- ⅔ cup whole milk
- ⅔ cup all-purpose flour
- ¼ cup canola oil
- 4 tablespoons (½ stick) butter
- ⅓ cup toasted sliced almonds
- 3 tablespoons fresh lemon juice
- 2 tablespoons minced parsley
- Salt and freshly ground pepper

Heat oven to 225°F.

Salt the fillets. In large skillet heat oil over medium-high heat. Put flour on a plate, add few grinds of pepper. Add milk to shallow bowl. When oil is shimmering, dip fillets in the milk then coat in flour. Fry fillets about 2 minutes per side till golden. Set fillets aside. Add butter and almonds to skillet. Whisk till butter starts to brown, about 4 minutes. Add lemon juice, stir. Plate the fish and pour sauce over fillets. Garnish with parsley, serve immediately.

Bourguignon de Paris *(Beef with wine)*

Makes 6 servings

- 8 ounces bacon, cut crosswise into ¼-inch strips or lardons
- 3 carrots, cut in ½-inch slices
- 3 large cloves garlic, minced
- 1 yellow onion, diced
- 2 tablespoons tomato paste
- 1 tablespoon sugar
- ¼ cup Cognac
- ½ cup flour
- 1 ½ teaspoons salt, divided
- 1 ½ teaspoons coarsely ground fresh pepper, divided
- 2 tablespoons olive oil
- 2 pounds chuck steak in 1-inch cubes
- 1 ½ cups good red wine
- 1 ½ cups beef broth
- 2 bay leaves
- 2 tablespoons fresh thyme leaves
- 2 tablespoons butter
- 8 ounces sliced white mushrooms
- 14 ounces frozen pearl onions

In a large Dutch oven or heavy pot combine the bacon, carrots, garlic, onion, tomato paste, sugar, and Cognac. Stir, cooking over medium heat till bacon is translucent and vegetables have softened, about 10 minutes. Transfer contents of pot to large bowl. Leave brown bits on bottom of pot to add flavor later.

In medium bowl stir together flour and 1 teaspoon each salt and pepper. Dredge meat in flour coating all completely. Add olive oil to Dutch oven over medium-high heat. Brown meat, in batches to avoid crowding, 15 minutes.

Reduce heat to medium and return bacon-vegetable mixture to pot with meat. Stir in wine, broth, bay leaves, thyme. Simmer, covered, over medium-low heat for one hour. Mixture likes to stick, stir frequently.

While meat cooks, in medium skillet, melt butter over medium-high heat. Add mushrooms and remaining ½ teaspoon each salt and pepper. Sauté till lightly browned, 6 to 8 minutes. Add mushrooms and pearl onions to pot and simmer, covered, for another hour. Make sure to stir, stir, stir. Serve over noodles with salad and crusty baguette.

Flamiche aux légumes *(Vegetable Tart)*

Makes 6 servings

Possibly the most delicious recipe in this book. Neck and neck with the fish tacos.

2 cups unbleached all-purpose flour

½ teaspoon sugar

10 tablespoons (1 ¼ sticks) cold butter in ½-inch cubes, and more for greasing pan

⅓ cup ice water

3 tablespoons olive oil

3 large, or 5 medium leeks, white parts only, halved lengthwise, sliced cross-wise (about 4 cups)

8 ounces sliced white mushrooms

10 ounces marinated artichoke hearts, drained and patted dry, roughly chopped

1 teaspoon dried thyme

2 large eggs

¼ cup heavy cream

¾ cup shredded Gruyere cheese (about 2 ounces)

Salt and freshly ground pepper

Make the pâte brisée (flaky tart dough). In mixing bowl whisk together flour, ½ teaspoon salt, sugar. Using your fingers work butter into flour till mixture is sandy and coarse. Add 3 tablespoons water, working it in till dough forms. If dough is dry, add more water, one tablespoon at a time. Shape dough into a disk, wrap in plastic, chill one hour.

On lightly floured surface, roll out dough into 14-inch circle. Add another teaspoon or two of water to make dough workable if needed. Transfer dough into a greased 11-inch tart pan, carefully easing in snugly, smoothing any tears or gaps. Trim dough to edge of pan or make standing rim for more rustic look. Set pan in fridge to chill while you prepare filling.

Heat oven to 425°F.

To large skillet add oil over medium-high heat. Add leeks, mushrooms, ½ teaspoon salt. Cook, stirring occasionally, till vegetables are lightly colored, 10 to 15 minutes. To the skillet add the artichokes, thyme, cook one minute more. Remove pan from heat.

In small bowl, whisk eggs with cream and cheese. Add egg mixture to vegetables in pan, season with 3 or 4 grinds fresh pepper and stir to combine.

Pour filling into tart pan. Bake 25 minutes till filling is set and crust is golden brown. Cool before serving. Is also delicious at room temperature.

Soufflé au Chocolat

Makes 4 soufflés

1 tablespoon butter, plus softened butter for ramekins	2 teaspoons of a nice bourbon
¼ cup sugar, divided	⅛ teaspoon cayenne pepper
1 tablespoon unbleached all-purpose flour	½ teaspoon salt
⅔ cup whole milk, room temperature	¼ teaspoon cream of tartar
4 ounces good quality bittersweet chocolate, chopped	Confectioners' sugar for garnish
2 egg yolks, 3 egg whites, room temperature *	* No yolk in whites whatsoever

Heat oven to 375°F.

Coat four 3 ½-inch ramekins generously with softened butter, 2 tablespoons sugar. Refrigerate. In a medium saucepan over medium heat melt 1 tablespoon butter. Add flour, whisking till combined, about 2 minutes. Add milk, whisking till mixture thickens, about 3 minutes. Remove pan from heat, add chocolate, wait one minute, stir. Add egg yolks, bourbon, cayenne, salt, whisk to combine.

In very clean medium bowl add egg whites and cream of tartar and whisk or beat with hand mixer till foamy. While beating, slowly add two tablespoons sugar till soft to firm peaks form. (See next page.) Fold ¼ of the egg whites gently into chocolate. Add the rest of egg whites, folding in completely but gently so as not to lose the volume.

Divide batter equally between the four ramekins, place on baking sheet, bake 11 to 14 minutes till soufflés rise. Serve immediately with a dusting of confectioners' sugar.

Bec D'oiseau

A soft to firm peak (not stiff) is known in French culinary parlance as a "bec d'oiseau," as it resembles the curve of a bird's beak.

Flower Arranging

Flower arranging is good fun. You just have to remember some basic ideas. 1) *Less is usually more.* Pick two to four types of flower and fern, holly, or other greenery total. Not too busy. 2) *Complementary colors, a contrast, or similars all work.* Yellow and purple are classic complements. White and red, a striking contrast. Pale colors together are beautiful. Even different flowers of a single color make a dramatic statement as well. 3) *Levels and depth.* Make sure heads of flowers are at different heights, and, just like decorating a Christmas tree, think about what's closest to the core of the arrangement versus what's projecting furthest outward. Create visual interest up and down and from inside to out. 4) *Occasion.* If it's Valentine's some red or pink roses might appeal. If Easter (my favorite for flower arrangements) yellow and lavender, other pastels. 5) *Texture, size, shape, line.* The variety of flowers you choose is important: contrast textures, sizes, shapes. Think of the overall "architectural" shape of your arrangement. Is it balanced, or angularly modern with a focus that's a bit off center? 6) Before arranging, always carefully slice ends of stems with sharp knife at an angle, to maximize "drinking" surface. Never scissors, they crush the stem ends closed.

Spring Carnival

HOLIDAY ITALIANO

Capesante alla Veneziana

Venetian Scallops

Makes 4 servings

Let's start this chapter in my favorite Italian town. Venice overflows with endless charms as well as a lot of great cooking. Unlike American scallop recipes, Venetian scallops are cooked through but not darkly seared.

1 ½ pounds sea scallops (about 16)

⅓ cup olive oil

4 cloves garlic, minced

⅓ cup dry white wine

Couple of dashes of your favorite hot sauce
   (this part is not Italian)

4 tablespoons chopped Italian parsley

Juice of 1 lemon

Salt and freshly ground pepper to taste

Wash scallops under cold water, pat dry with towels so they don't spatter too much when you put them in hot oil. In large skillet, over medium heat, heat oil till shimmering. Add garlic, cook one minute, stirring. Increase heat to medium-high, add scallops, wine, sprinkle with hot sauce, salt and pepper.

Cook five minutes each side. Divide scallops among four serving plates, 4 per plate. Add parsley and lemon juice to pan sauce, cook one minute, serve with parsley-lemon sauce spooned over scallops.

Polpette di Carne with Ragù Veloce *(Meatballs with Quick Ragù)*

Makes 4 to 6 servings

- 2 tablespoons olive oil
- 1 medium onion, diced
- 1 large or 2 medium ribs celery, diced
- 1 medium carrot, diced
- 1 large clove garlic, minced
- 1 can (28 ounces) whole peeled plum tomatoes, with liquid, coarsely chopped (authentic San Marzano preferred)
- 1 bay leaf
- 2 teaspoons salt, divided
- 1 pound ground beef
- ¾ pound ground pork
- ½ teaspoon freshly ground pepper
- ½ cup panko breadcrumbs
- ⅓ cup shredded Pecorino Romano
- 1 large egg
- 3 tablespoons minced fresh basil
- 3 tablespoons minced parsley

In Dutch oven or heavy pot heat oil over medium-high heat. Add the Italian soffritto (onion, celery, carrot) and garlic, and cook till softened, about 5 minutes. Add tomatoes to pot, break up with wooden spoon. Add bay leaf and 1 teaspoon salt. Partially cover, bring mixture to boil, reduce heat to simmer for 20 minutes.

While sauce simmers, in large bowl, combine beef, pork, breadcrumbs, cheese, egg, basil, parsley, remaining teaspoon salt, pepper. Add ½ cup of sauce to meat, mix all together with fork till well combined. Shape mixture into 16 balls, about 2 inches in diameter. Gently place meatballs in sauce without stirring. Return sauce to gentle simmer, cover and cook for 20 to 25 minutes. Test a meatball to make sure is cooked through. Remove bay leaf, serve.

Pesce Lombardo

Makes 4 servings

- 4 large sole or flounder fillets, about 1 ½ pounds total
- ¼ cup white wine
- 1 teaspoon salt
- 1 small shallot, diced
- 2 large eggs
- 1 ½ cups panko breadcrumbs
- 3 tablespoons minced cooked ham
- 2 teaspoons freshly ground pepper
- 4 tablespoons (½ stick) butter, divided
- 1 tablespoons canola oil
- 3 tablepoons finely chopped flat-leaf parsley
- Lemon wedges

In large baking dish place the fillets. Pour wine over them, then sprinkle on the salt and shallot, distributing evenly. Let sit at room temperature for 15 minutes.

To a wide shallow bowl, add eggs, beat lightly. To a second shallow bowl or plate, add panko, ham, pepper, stir to combine. One at a time, brush shallots off fish, coat both sides of fillets with egg. Then dredge in panko mixture, patting coating on firmly. In large nonstick skillet over medium-high heat, heat 2 tablespoons butter and 1 tablespoon canola oil. Cook fillets two at a time, turning once, about 3 minutes each side depending on thickness of fillets. Add remaining 2 tablespoons butter, cook last two fillets. Serve with garnish of parsley, and lemon wedges.

NATIONAL
MEATBALL DAY:
MARCH 9

Spaghetti alla Carbonara

Makes 4 servings

1 tablespoon salt
12 ounces spaghetti
4 ounces guanciale , otherwise pancetta or thick cut
  smoked bacon, sliced in ¼" cubes or strips
3 large egg yolks, 1 large whole egg
½ cup grated Pecorino Romano, more for garnish
3 grinds medium-coarse ground pepper

To medium pot, add water, 1 tablespoon salt, bring to boil. Add spaghetti (do not break it in half!) and cook till al dente. Meanwhile, in large skillet, over medium-high heat, begin cooking guanciale/pancetta, stirring frequently till slightly browned ("rosolare" in Italian), not crisp. Reduce heat to low. In medium bowl, lightly beat eggs, add cheese, 3 grinds of pepper, stir all together with a fork till well combined.

When spaghetti is al dente, grab with the tongs in a series of bunches from the pot and place in the nearby skillet with the guanciale/pancetta. Toss to coat with fat and flavor. Remove skillet from heat and let cool for 2 minutes, stirring. Now add the egg mixture and stir briskly, using the tongs. Finish with a few more grinds of pepper and serve.

Pasta e fagioli *(Pasta Fazool)*

Makes 8 to 10 servings

1 pound dried borlotti beans (aka cranberry/Roman)
¼ cup olive oil
½ pound pancetta or bacon, cut in cubes/strips
2 medium onions, chopped
3 medium carrots, unpeeled, in ½-inch slices
3 ribs celery, in ½-inch slices
2 cloves garlic, chopped
¾ cup of a nice prosecco

1 can (14 ounces) whole peeled tomatoes
2 sprigs fresh rosemary
2 bay leaves
1 smoked pig knuckle or hock
4 cups chicken broth
2 tablespoons chopped parsley
2 cups ditalini, small shells, or elbows
Coarsely ground pepper

To large pot, add beans, cover with water by 3 inches and soak 10 to 12 hours, or overnight. They should absorb most of the water.

In a Dutch oven, over medium-high heat, bring oil to just shimmering. Add pancetta, onions, carrots, celery, garlic. Cook till softened but not taking on color, about 7 minutes.

Add prosecco, to deglaze and "insaporire" (flavor) the pancetta onion mixture, cooking for 4 minutes till alcohol reduced by half. Break up tomatoes by hand as you add to soup. Add rosemary, bay leaves, pig knuckle, beans, broth, 3 cups water, and stir.

Bring Dutch oven contents to a simmer and cook uncovered for about 1 hour 30 minutes or till beans are tender but retain a bit of a bite. While beans are simmering, cook pasta in water with 1 tablespoon salt till al dente. Set aside. Remove rosemary stems and bay leaves from beans.

Add the parsley, cooked pasta, a few coarse grinds of pepper, cook for 3 minutes more. Serve with a crusty Italian bread and a sprinkle of Parmesan cheese.

Sugo Rosso San Marco

Makes 3 ½ cups sauce

2 cloves garlic, minced
1 green bell pepper, diced
1 sweet onion, diced
1 large carrot, diced

1 tablespoon olive oil
1 tablespoon dried oregano
1 teaspoon sugar
1 bay leaf
12 ounces tomato paste
28 ounces tomato sauce

In a medium Dutch oven or stew pot, heat oil over medium-high heat. Add vegetable mixture and cook till slightly colored, about 3 minutes.

Add oregano and sugar, stir, and reduce heat to medium. Add tomato paste, combine with vegetables for 1 minute, stir in tomato sauce and add bay leaf. Simmer over medium to low heat, stirring frequently, 10 minutes. Don't dry it out. Be sure to partially cover as sauce may splatter. Taste and adjust with salt and pepper as desired.

Serve over pasta with a sprinkle of Parmesan, or as part of another recipe. Look forward to unbridled praise and perhaps an operatic aria or two.

Chicken Parmigiana with Sugo Rosso San Marco   *Makes 6 servings*

1 ½ cups flour
2 teaspoons each salt and pepper
3 large eggs
1 ½ cups panko breadcrumbs
2 tablespoons minced flat-leaf parsley
1 teaspoon dried oregano

1 ¼ cups shredded Parmesan cheese, divided
1 cup olive oil
6 thin-sliced chicken cutlets, about 2 pounds
2 cups Sugo Rosso San Marco
6 slices fresh mozzerella, ¼-inch thick
3 tablespoons fresh basil, chopped

Heat oven to 375°F. Line a sheet pan with parchment paper, set aside. In a large plate or wide shallow bowl, whisk together 1 ½ cups flour, salt, and pepper. In a second bowl, lightly beat eggs. In a third bowl, combine panko, ¾ cup shredded Parmesan, parsley, and oregano, whisk.

One at a time, pat cutlets dry, coat both sides in flour mixture, shake off excess. Dip both sides in egg, then dredge in panko mixture, making sure they are entirely coated. Set aside on prepared sheet pan.

In large skillet, heat ⅓ cup of oil over medium-high heat till it shimmers. Working in batches of two cutlets at a time, cook till golden brown on both sides, about 3 minutes each side. Add another ⅓ cup oil for each two as you go. Chicken should be an internal temperature of 165°F when done.

In a 9 x 13-inch baking dish, spread 1 cup of the sauce. Add cutlets in a single layer, overlapping slightly if needed. Cover with remaining sauce. Sprinkle with remaining Parmesan. In the center of each cutlet, place a slice of mozzerella. Bake uncovered on upper rack for 15 minutes till cutlets are hot and cheese is melted and lightly browned. Garnish with chopped basil and stand back as the hungry mob invades!

Ragù alla Bolognese

Makes 6 servings

Suffuses the house with a revitalizing Italian bouquet. You're sure to have, a lovely, bella notte.

- 1 ½ pounds half ground beef & ground pork
- 7 ounces uncured ham, in ¼-inch cubes
- 2 tablespoons olive oil
- 1 large onion, chopped fine
- 3 big carrots, chopped fine
- 5 ribs celery, chopped fine
- 4 cloves garlic, minced
- 1 teaspoon dried oregano
- 1 teaspoon ground coriander
- 1 teaspoon coarsely ground fresh pepper
- 18 ounces good quality tomato paste
- 2 bay leaves
- 2 cups your favorite white wine

In a large deep skillet, over medium-high heat, add beef, pork, ham. Cook till meat no longer pink, about 7 minutes. Push meat to side of skillet, add 2 tablespoons olive oil. Add onion, carrots, celery, garlic, oregano, coriander, pepper. Cook till vegetables have softened, 5 minutes.

Add tomato paste, cook 3 minutes, stirring all meat and vegetables together. Add bay leaves, wine. Stir over medium heat to cook off a bit of wine, 5 minutes. Add 1 cup water. Stir in till it incorporates and is reduced then stir in 1 more cup. Simmer on low heat for an hour. Add a third cup of water after 30 minutes then more if appears necessary.

Lasagna Florentine with Ragù alla Bolognese

Makes 6 to 8 servings

- 15 ounces ricotta cheese
- 2 large eggs
- 1 teaspoon salt, divided
- ½ teaspoon freshly ground pepper
- 1 teaspoon dried oregano
- 1 cup shredded Parmesan cheese, divided
- 1 cup shredded mozzerella, divided
- 4 tablespoons olive oil, divided
- 1 tablespoon butter
- 4 cloves garlic, 2 peeled, 2 minced, divided
- 9 ounces flat-leaf spinach
- 1 medium zucchini, sliced thin
- 8 ounces sliced white mushrooms
- 5 to 6 cups Ragù alla Bolognese
- 1 package (8.8 ounces) no-boil lasagna noodles
- Chiffonade of fresh basil for garnish

Heat oven to 350°F. In a medium bowl, stir together ricotta, eggs, ½ teaspoon salt, pepper, oregano, ½ cup Parmesan, ½ cup mozzerella. Mix well, set aside.

In large skillet, over medium heat, heat 1 tablespoon each olive oil and butter, 2 whole peeled cloves garlic. Cook spinach 2 to 3 minutes till just wilted, set aside. Add remaining 2 tablespoons oil to skillet, increase to medium-high heat, cook zucchini, minced garlic, and mushrooms with remaining ½ teaspoon salt till softened, 8 minutes. Set aside with spinach.

In a 9 x 13-inch baking dish, spread thin layer of bolognese sauce. Cover with 4 lasagna noodles, breaking up if necessary to line dish. Spread with ½ remaining sauce. Next, layer ½ the ricotta and egg mixture, followed by ½ the spinach and vegetables. Top with four more noodles, then last of ricotta, rest of vegetables, rest of sauce. Top this with remaining half ricotta, Parmesan, and mozzerella. Bake, covered, 30 minutes. Uncover another 15 minutes to brown top. Garnish with basil.

Rosemary Focaccia *"La Migliore del Mondo"*

Makes about 9 servings

1 tablespoon sugar

1 package (¼-ounce) active dry yeast

6 cups unbleached all-purpose flour, plus more for working dough

2 tablespoons coarse or kosher salt, divided

1 cup olive oil, divided

2 tablespoons chopped fresh rosemary

To small bowl add 1 ½ cups warm water and sugar. What's warm? It should feel to the touch like it's the right temperature to take a shower in (103°F to 105°F). Add yeast, stir vigorously and cover for 5 to 7 minutes till foamy.

To a large bowl, add flour and 1 tablespoon salt, whisk.

Add yeast mixture and ½ cup olive oil, mix ingredients together with your hand till dough forms. It should start out shaggy then come together quickly, about 3 minutes.

Flour your hands if dough is tacky. On lightly floured counter, knead for another 10 minutes till dough is smooth. Form into a ball, coat the inside of a medium bowl with 1 tablespoon oil, roll dough in oil and cover bowl with dark cloth, set in warm area to rise. It should double in size in an hour to 90 minutes.

Coat a half sheet pan (13 x 18 inches) with ¼ cup olive oil. Place dough in pan and smooth out to an even layer touching edges of pan. Turn dough over once to coat other side with oil. Cover pan with dark cloth or plastic wrap and let dough rise to about twice the size, 30 minutes to 1 hour.

Heat oven to 400°F.

Make indentations with fingertips about an inch apart across surface of dough. Press your fingers down to touch pan but don't make holes through the dough. Brush or drizzle dough with 3 tablespoons oil, then top with a even sprinkling of fresh rosemary.

Bake until golden brown, 18 to 22 minutes.

Nonna's Rainbow Cookie Carnevale

Makes about 32 cookies. Store them covered in fridge.

2 ½ sticks softened butter, more for pans

4 large eggs, whites and yolks separated

½ teaspoon salt

1 package (7 ounces) almond paste, broken up

1 cup sugar

½ teaspoon vanilla extract

½ teaspoon almond extract

2 cups unbleached all-purpose flour

Red and green food coloring (liquid or gel)

1 ½ cups raspberry preserves

9 ounces high quality semisweet chocolate, chopped

1 cup heavy cream

¼ cup (½ stick) butter for chocolate layers, divided

FOR MORE ITALIAN FARE, LOOK FOR THE FEAST OF THE SEVEN FISHES IN THE CHRISTMAS CHAPTER

Heat oven to 350°F. Butter three 9 x 13-inch baking pans, cut parchment paper to line bottom and long sides of pans. Then butter the paper.

In a clean, dry, medium bowl, add egg whites and salt, beat with electric mixer till stiff peaks form.

In large bowl, add almond paste, sugar, vanilla, and almond extracts, work together with fingers till sandy, about 4 minutes. Add butter and beat with electric mixer till fluffy, about 2 minutes. Add yolks and beat till fully incorporated. Using a spatula or spoon, fold in flour, till just combined. Fold in half of egg whites mixture gently but thoroughly, repeat with other half. Divide batter evenly among three bowls, coloring first with about 25 drops liquid red food coloring, the next with 25 drops green, and the third leave plain. (If using gel coloring about two squirts each should do.)

Place a different color batter into each of the three prepared pans, spreading in a thin even layer edge to edge. You can use an offset spatula to do this, I also like using a teaspoon.

Bake about 12 minutes, rotating once between shelves in oven, till cake is just set in center. Do not overbake. Using edges of parchment liners, lift cakes out of pans, cool on racks or counter.

Place green layer back into a single parchment-covered sheet pan. Spread with half preserves. Line up white layer on top of that. Spread white layer with remaining half preserves, top with red layer. Cover tightly with plastic wrap, place another sheet pan on top. Weight this with a glass baking dish or stack of bowls, etc. Refrigerate for 5 hours, or overnight.

Unweight and unwrap cake. Chop up half the chocolate, place in bowl. Heat ½ cup heavy cream, pour over chocolate, stir. Add two tablespoons butter, stir. Pour on cake, spread evenly. Let sit in fridge to firm up, at least 1 hour. Flip, repeat with other half chocolate, cool. Chill overnight, covered in plastic.

Place on cutting board, green layer up, trim edges with serrated knife. With sharp chef's knife cut in four longwise pieces. Cut crosswise into cookies as desired.

Gabriele Corcos, Italian celebrity cook, entrepreneur, and television personality, is creator, host, and producer of the Cooking Channel's *Extra Virgin,* in which he appears with his equally talented wife, Debi Mazar.

He is a native of Tuscany and author of the *New York Times* best-selling cookbook, Extra Virgin. Gabriele has been made a Knight by the Italian President of the Republic, in recognition of his outstanding work promoting Italian heritage in the USA. It is Italy's highest civilian honor.

Simple food. Salt and pepper.

What is your favorite food region of Italy and why? You are from Fiesole.

The thing about Italy, we do appreciate food from other regions. But there is this very natural attachment to your own land. So my favorite is for sure Tuscan food. Simple food. Salt and pepper. Few seasonings. Lots of grill. Lots of charcoal. Lots of fire. The islands have a lot to offer. Oh, for God's sakes. Summer in the islands. Being able to fish and cook on the same day. It keeps me in touch with the world, with nature, and with the kitchen.

What's your favorite recipe? If you had to choose one most delicious dish, or that represents the region.

What I appreciate of Tuscan cuisine and Italy is the

way ingredients are enjoyed as ingredients. So a meat carpaccio. A fish carpaccio. A tuna tartare. A beef tartare. A good fire, a good bottle of wine. To me, it's not about the specific recipe.

Really the purity of the ingredients.

The best ones you can get.

Do you ever change up Italian recipes?

One of the things that I love to do is tacos.

Italian tacos?

No, in the US, when I have leftover roast beef, or steak, or fried chicken, it ends up in tacos. In Tuscany, we turn leftovers into soups or stews. I like chowder. I developed my own recipe, with fish and clams from the Italian coast. No bacon. Guanciale.

Who was the best cook in your family when you were growing up?

Oh, it depends on things. My mother was the comfort of the home. So it really did not matter the quality of the food. It came with hugs and smiles. And that was okay. But Grandma was better.

Lola.

Lola was better than Mom. Everybody knew it [laughter]. There was always a feast. The fact is that our family was weird because my father came from a mixed Jewish family where the mother was Catholic and my grandfather was Jewish. But neither converted, so my father ended up growing into a kosher house and kitchen. My mother came from a mixed marriage, but my grandmother was a Catholic from Venice, and she refused to convert in order to marry my grandfather. They were desperately in love, but she's like, "Look, I'm staying the way that I am. Take it or leave it." And it was okay with my grandfather. So on one side, I have a kosher father, on the other, a mother that came from a kitchen that had a Catholic and a Jew, but there was pork, and it was mixed. So when the families got together for holidays, it was always like a fine balance of figuring out what is Italian kosher?

In your books, I really like your introductions to the kitchen and the pantry. Any hints?

Never overstock your fridge. Never buy more food than you need. Aside from the waste, it takes away the spontaneity that is very, very important to eating healthy.

What's your favorite holiday and what's the main dish you like to make most to celebrate it?

Eggplant Parmesan for New Year's Eve. Big occasion. I do an extra batch so we always have leftovers.

Any tips on grocery shopping?

I never shop hungry. Never. And know your stores. The meat is always better at the butcher. The bread is always better at the bakery.

Anything else come to mind in terms of what you want America's home cooks to think about?

Think about the relationships you develop with the people you buy food from. Try to feel connected. Feeling connected with the food you eat makes you a better cook. It makes you aware. So there are mistakes. Just go for it. I believe that people who have even minimal skills very often should just look at a recipe then, if they know the ingredients, if they know their way around the kitchen, there is always a way to own a recipe, to express yourself. I usually only look at the title and the picture of the recipe. Good pictures really speak to me. I'm like, "I can do this. I can get there."

Throw Me Something, Mister! A Mardi Gras Jamboree

Shrimp Rémoulade Rue Royale

Makes 6 to 8 servings

This is a tart and tangy rémoulade blanche, lighter in color than the rémoulade rouge one sees in New Orleans restaurants.

- ¼ cup good quality mayonnaise
- ⅓ cup Creole or spicy coarse-grained mustard
- 2 tablespoons ketchup
- ¾ cup chopped scallions (white and green parts)
- ½ cup celery, chopped fine
- ⅓ cup parsley, chopped fine
- ¼ cup finely minced kosher dill pickles or cornichons
- 2 tablespoons prepared horseradish
- 1 tablespoon red wine vinegar plus 2 teaspoons
- ½ cup canola oil plus 1 tablespoon
- 1 teaspoon coarsely ground black pepper
- 1 small head iceberg lettuce, quartered, cut in thin shreds
- 48 large cleaned shrimp, tails removed, cooked

In large bowl, thoroughly combine mayo, mustard, ketchup, scallions, celery, parsley, pickles, horseradish, 1 tablespoon vinegar, ½ cup oil, black pepper. Toss together with shrimp, chill overnight, tightly covered. To dress lettuce: in small bowl whisk together 1 tablespoon oil and 2 teaspoons vinegar, toss to combine. Divide lettuce among six salad plates and top with Shrimp Rémoulade.

Petit Filet and Fish Yvonne *à la Galatoire's*

Makes 4 servings. Crabmeat Yvonne tops either meat or fish in this recipe.

For Crabmeat Yvonne: **4 ounces (1 stick) butter**

Meat: **Four 6-ounce petit filet mignons, rest 30 minutes at room temperature and generously season with coarse salt and pepper all sides.**

For Meat: **¼ cup canola oil and 2 tablespoons butter, 2 cloves garlic, 4 thyme sprigs**

OR Fish: **Four 6-ounce fillets of flounder or any other lean fish like drum, sole. Salt and pepper both sides.**

For fish: **¼ cup canola oil and 1 cup flour seasoned with 2 teaspoons salt and 1 teaspoon pepper**

To finish the Yvonne topping:

> **8 ounces sliced white mushrooms (about 2 ½ cups)**
> **1 cup roughly chopped marinated artichoke hearts**
> **1 cup chopped scallions, white and green parts, divided**
> **½ pound lump crabmeat**
> **1 tablespoon lemon juice**
> **2 teaspoons red wine vinegar**

Heat oven to 225°F. *Make brown butter for Crabmeat Yvonne:* in a small saucepan over medium to medium-low heat, melt 1 stick butter and whisk continuously till dark brown but not burnt, about 6 minutes, set aside.

Petit Filets: in a medium skillet over high heat, add oil, garlic. Heat till shimmering and sear seasoned filets on all sides, about 4 minutes total. Add butter and thyme, baste with pan juices. Cook another 2 minutes for rare, 4 minutes for medium-rare. Tent with foil on sheet pan and keep filets warm in oven.

Fish: coat in seasoned flour on both sides. In a non-stick skillet over medium-high heat add oil. When shimmering, brown fish till golden, 4 minutes first side, flip, brown 2 more minutes. Set aside tented with foil.

To finish the Yvonne: wipe out pan, add brown butter (with sediment). Over medium-high heat, add mushrooms, artichokes, ⅔ cup scallions, cook till softened, about 3 minutes. Add crabmeat, lemon juice, vinegar, heat through, 2 minutes. Top petit filets or fish with Yvonne, garnish with ⅓ cup scallions and serve immediately.

Pirate Alley Gumbo

Makes 12 servings

Ahoy matey! No need to walk the plank today! Named for the famous passage next to Saint Louis Cathedral, this gumbo's a standout due to the rare addition of white fish. Lifelong New Orleanians give it an enthusiastic three thumbs up! (Wait, where'd that third thumb come from?)

2 tablespoons plus ¼ cup canola oil
1 pound fresh okra, ends trimmed, cut in ½-inch pieces
Heaping ¼ cup all-purpose flour
1 large onion, chopped
4 ribs celery, chopped
1 green bell pepper, chopped
5 cloves garlic, minced
2 teaspoons fresh thyme leaves
3 ½ cups chicken broth (with salt)
2 bay leaves

½ teaspoon each ground nutmeg, ginger
½ teaspoon cayenne pepper
1 (28 ounces) can crushed tomatoes
1 ½ pounds firm white fish: cod, bass, grouper or snapper, cut in ¾-inch cubes
½ pound lump crabmeat, cleaned
1 teaspoon gumbo filé
Cooked rice for serving

In Dutch oven or heavy pot, heat 2 tablespoons oil over medium-high heat. Add okra, cook, stirring occasionally till bright green, about 4 minutes. Transfer to plate, set okra aside. Wipe loose remains out of the pot. Make the roux: to Dutch oven, over medium heat, add ¼ cup oil. When oil is hot add flour. Whisk constantly for 5 to 10 minutes till you have a peanut butter-colored roux.

Add the trinity of onion, celery, bell pepper plus garlic, cook till softened about 3 minutes. Stir in thyme, cook 1 minute more. Add broth, deglaze pot. Add bay leaves, nutmeg, ginger, cayenne, tomatoes. Stir to combine, bring to a simmer, partially cover. Cook gently over low heat till thickened and reduced by about a third, 35 minutes, stirring frequently. Add fish, crabmeat, cooked okra. Simmer till fish is cooked through, 6 to 8 minutes. Do not boil.

Remove bay leaves, stir in filé. Let rest 15 minutes before serving. Spoon over hot rice with your number one hot sauce at the ready. Even better the next day.

85

Bon Ton Muffuletta

Makes 6 servings

If Bon Ton Café's salad dressing and Central Grocery's muffuletta had a baby.

- 1 cup diced pimento-stuffed olives
- ¾ cup diced pitted Kalamata olives
- ¾ cup diced giardiniera
- 2 tablespoons minced shallot
- 1 teaspoon minced garlic
- 2 tablespoons Creole or spicy coarse-grained mustard
- 1 tablespoon Worcestershire sauce
- ¼ cup grated Parmesan cheese

- 1 tablespoon prepared horseradish
- ⅓ cup olive oil
- 1 teaspoon dried oregano
- 1 tablespoon dried parsley
- 1 large loaf Italian bread, with sesame seeds
- 1 package (4 ounces) sliced Genoa salami
- 1 package (4 ounces) sliced mortadella
- 1 package (4 ounces) sliced provolone cheese

In a medium bowl, combine the olives, giardiniera, shallot, garlic, mustard, Worcestershire, Parmesan, horseradish, olive oil, oregano, parsley. Chill 1 hour for flavors to blend.

Spread bottom half of bread with half the olive salad. Layer on salami, then mortadella, then salami, then mortadella, then provolone. Top with rest of salad, close sandwich, wrap in plastic, let sit for 45 minutes at room temperature before serving. Unwrap and slice.

French Quarter Red Beans and Rice

Makes 8 servings

Red beans and rice is traditionally served on Mondays, but I eat it every day. This recipe is for red kidneys, not smaller red beans. The latter cook faster. Extra credit: if you have a big old ham bone, include it while cooking, for extra yum.

- 1 pound dried red kidney beans, picked over and rinsed
- 3 tablespoons olive oil
- 1 large onion, diced
- 4 to 5 ribs celery, diced

- 1 large green bell pepper, diced
- 3 cloves garlic, minced
- 2 bay leaves
- 1 scant teaspoon cayenne pepper
- 2 teaspoons fresh thyme leaves
- 7 or 8 ounces ham steak cut in ½-inch cubes
- 12 ounces andouille sausage, cut in ½-inch slices
- ¼ cup (½ stick) butter
- Cooked white or brown rice

To a large Dutch oven add beans and 10 cups water, bring to boil for 10 minutes. Remove from heat and let soak in water another 50 minutes.

Meanwhile, in large skillet, heat oil over medium-high heat till shimmering. Add onion, celery, bell pepper, garlic, bay leaves. Stir together and cook till vegetables soften, about 6 minutes. Add cayenne, thyme, ham, sausage, cook till vegetables are tender and meat is heated through, about 10 more minutes. Stir meat and vegetable mixture into pot with beans and water.

Bring to a full boil, then reduce to a simmer over low heat. Cook, uncovered, stirring every 10 or 15 minutes, about one hour or till beans are tender. If mixture is sticking to the bottom of pot, your heat is too high. Remove bay leaves, stir in butter, and cook 5 minutes more.

Serve over your favorite rice, with a side of grilled sausage or chicken fingers, and a hunk or two of French bread!

Stella's Creole Meatloaf

Makes 6 to 8 servings

Keep the Stanley in your life coming back for more.

2 tablespoons butter

2 cloves garlic, minced

1 medium onion, chopped fine

3 ribs celery, chopped fine

1 green bell pepper, chopped fine

1 heaping tablespoon fresh thyme leaves

1 ½ tablespoons Creole seasoning (with salt), divided

2 pounds ground beef

1 cup panko breadcrumbs

1 ½ teaspoons cayenne pepper

2 large eggs lightly beaten

⅓ cup ketchup

¼ cup milk

Heat oven to 375°F. Line 9 x 5-inch loaf pan with foil.

In large skillet over medium-high heat, melt butter. Add garlic, the trinity of onion, celery, bell pepper, and cook till softened, about 4 minutes. Add thyme and ½ tablespoon Creole seasoning, cook 4 minutes longer.

In large bowl, combine meat, panko, cooked trinity, remaining 1 tablespoon Creole seasoning, cayenne, eggs, ketchup, milk. Using hands, mix together thoroughly.

Pack meat mixture into prepared loaf pan, invert onto a foil-lined sheet pan. Remove loaf pan and foil lining from molded meat.

Bake on upper shelf of oven for 1 hour to an internal temp of 160°F.

Ignatius's Hot Dog Jambalaya

Makes 10 Servings

3 tablespoons butter

10 all beef hot dogs (about 16 ounces), cut in ½-inch slices

1 large onion, diced

2 ribs celery, diced

1 medium green bell pepper, diced

2 cloves garlic, minced

1 teaspoon fresh thyme leaves

1 can (16 ounces) petite diced tomatoes

1 can (6 ounces) tomato paste

1 cup chicken broth

2 tablespoons minced parsley

1 pound medium to large shrimp, peeled, deveined

2 cups cooked wild rice blend

1 tablespoon ground smoked paprika

1 tablespoon salt

1 teaspoon sugar

½ teaspoon freshly ground pepper

½ teaspoon cayenne pepper

In Dutch oven or large pot, melt butter over medium heat. Cook hot dogs, browning both sides, about 10 minutes. Set dogs aside on paper towel-lined plate.

Add onion, celery, bell pepper, garlic, thyme to pot, reduce heat to medium, cook till softened, about 5 minutes.

Add tomatoes, tomato paste, broth, parsley. Cook 3 minutes, stirring frequently.

Add hot dogs, cook 2 minutes. Add shrimp, stir till pink, 3 minutes. Mix in rice, paprika, salt, sugar, black pepper, cayenne, stir thoroughly. Cook 5 minutes uncovered till rice is heated through, stirring frequently. Serve hot!

FEAST DAY OF
SAINT EXPEDITE:
APRIL 19

Pound Cake for Saint Expedite

Makes 8 servings

Expedite, a Christian martyr and Roman soldier of lore, is revered in French Catholic and Creole culture in New Orleans as the saint of speedy cases or "urgent and just causes." His word is "hodie," because he chose his Christianity "today." Frequently petitioned with prayers to bestow money and work, he is good at making all kinds of things happen in dire situations, as long as you light a candle for him and promise him gifts such as water, wine, flowers, and most importantly, his pound cake. His colors are red, white, and yellow, and he likes odd numbers. It has also been the custom, after your petition is granted and you bestow your freshly baked cake, to thank the saint by buying a classified listing in the paper. The saint likes attention. These days, you can just post your thanks on social media. And, did you know, when you bake a pound cake or a cornbread, the crack in the top is a sign of good luck? Well now you do.

- **2 cups unbleached all-purpose flour**
- **1 teaspoon baking powder**
- **½ teaspoon salt**
- **1 cup butter (2 sticks), room temperature**
- **1 cup sugar**
- **5 large eggs**
- **1 teaspoon vanilla extract**
- **1 cup whole milk**

Heat oven to 350°F. Grease and flour a 9 x 5-inch loaf pan.

In medium bowl, whisk together flour, baking powder, salt. In a large bowl, cream together butter and sugar, beating till fluffy, at least 2 minutes. Beat in eggs, one at a time, then vanilla. In three additions each, add dry ingredients, alternating with milk. Beat till batter is smooth. Pour batter into prepared pan, bake one hour or till golden brown and a toothpick comes out clean.

ROUX Oil or bacon fat, plus flour, stirred constantly over medium heat till it darkens in color. Used as a base for gumbo-type dishes. Creole is lighter in tone, Cajun dark. Process can take a bit of time. Refill your wine glass first or you'll roux the day.

Saint Joseph's Lily
(Pane di San Giuseppe)

The Feast of Saint Joseph is a cherished Italian holiday in New Orleans. Altars with decorative breads and zeppole (pastries) are put out all over town to celebrate the saint's feast day, March 19. The "carpenter of Nazareth" is commemorated with hammers and other tools crafted from bread. He also, according to lore, had a staff that blossomed into a lily to signify he was special among men. Unlike a Saint Joseph's sculpture that is meant to be on display for several days, this pane (bread) is made to be enjoyed right out of the oven. It is tender in texture and delicately sweet.

1 cup very warm water (103°F to 105°F)

½ teaspoon sugar

1 package (¼-ounce) active dry yeast

2 large eggs, divided

3 tablespoons honey

½ teaspoon anise extract

1 teaspoon salt

3 ¼ cups unbleached flour, divided

2 tablespoons salted butter, softened

1 tablespoon canola oil

¼ cup sesame seeds

To a small bowl add the warm water and sugar. Add yeast, stir vigorously and cover with dark towel for 5 to 7 minutes till foamy. To large mixing bowl add yeast mixture, 1 lightly beaten egg, honey, anise extract, salt, and 1 cup flour. With a large spoon mix vigorously till fully blended, 2 minutes. Add butter, mashing against side of bowl to help incorporate fully. Add another 2 cups flour, stir, forming soft sticky dough. On lightly floured surface, knead dough till stretchy and smooth, about 5 minutes. It will still be sticky. If too sticky, add 1 or 2 tablespoons more flour. Wipe out mixing bowl and coat with oil. Place dough in bowl, turning to coat all sides with oil. Cover with dark towel and set to rise in a warm place till dough doubles in volume, 1 to 2 hours.

Line a sheet pan with parchment paper. Shape dough into a large lily with stem and leaves (see photograph for one approach). Cover lily with a towel and let rest another 30 minutes. Dough will increase again in size. Now refine and sculpt the petals and leaves a bit more to your vision.

Heat oven to 400°F. Brush top of lily all over with 1 lightly beaten egg and evenly cover with sesame seeds. Bake for 25 minutes till golden brown. Cool on rack.

Chef Leah's kitchen

With Chef Leah's grandson, Chef Trevor

Creole Wiener Spaghetti z'Herbes

Dedicated to Chef Leah Chase, Queen of Creole Cuisine

Makes 8 servings

This recipe is inspired by two landmark dishes from the legendary career of Chef Leah Chase: her first hot lunch in the Quarter, "Creole Wiener Spaghetti," and her famous Holy Thursday "Gumbo z'Herbes" at Dooky Chase's. The nine herbes are an odd number, for good luck. That's how many new friends you'll make after you eat this tasty dish!

2 ½ tablespoons canola oil

12 ounces andouille sausage, cut in ¼-inch slices

2 tablespoons all-purpose flour

1 medium onion, diced

2 ribs celery, diced

1 green bell pepper, diced

2 cloves garlic, minced

2 teaspoons fresh thyme leaves

These are the greens, or z'herbes. For collard greens, mustard greens, and chard, tear leaves away from stems and chop leaves bite-size. For all greens, firmly pack to measure. Combine all in large bowl.

2 cups chopped collard greens

2 cups chopped mustard greens

2 cups chopped red chard

2 cups chopped romaine, crunchy bottoms cut off

2 cups chopped spinach

2 cups chopped arugula

1 cup chopped carrot tops (save the carrots for an Italian soffritto!)

1 cup chopped parsley

2 cups chopped broccoli rabe, no stems

1 tablespoon paprika

1 can (28 ounces) crushed tomatoes

1 tablespoon salt

1 teaspoon sugar

1 teaspoon filé powder

1 pound spaghetti, cooked, with your choice of a popular Louisiana hot sauce nearby

To Dutch oven or large pot, add oil over medium-high heat. Add andouille, cook till lightly browned. Transfer sausage to paper towel-lined plate. To fat, in pot over medium-low heat, add flour, whisking constantly till a peanut butter-colored roux forms, 8 to 10 minutes.

Add onion, celery, bell pepper, garlic, thyme. Cook, stirring with wooden spoon till softened, about 4 minutes. Lots of flavorful bits (fond, gradoux) will stick on bottom of pot to scrape up later.

Over medium heat, add greens by handfuls to onion mixture, stirring and scraping bottom of pot after each addition till all are wilted. Cook till greens are collapsed and steaming, about 10 minutes. Add paprika, cook 1 minute, add tomatoes, salt, sugar, and return andouille to pot. Stir all to combine.

Bring to gentle simmer, cook, uncovered, till greens are tender but still have a bit of crunch, about 20 minutes. Stir in filé powder and serve over spaghetti. As you serve, do a Chef Leah-inspired dance of love.

EASTER PRIMAVERA

Pizza Primavera

Makes 6 servings

This one's for the vegetarians in the audience, but you can do whatever you want with this dough it's very flexible! Tomato sauce, cheese, pepperoni! I add arugula with vinaigrette to top it off.

24 stalks fresh asparagus, sliced in 1-inch pieces
10 ounces multicolored heirloom tomatoes, sliced in half
8 ounces sliced white mushrooms
1 jar (12 ounces) marinated artichoke hearts, sliced, reserve marinade
3 cups all-purpose flour
2 cups 5 percent Greek yogurt
3 teaspoons baking powder
1 teaspoon smoked paprika
1 teaspoon oregano
1 teaspoon chili powder
8 ounces mozzarella, shredded

4 ounces Parmesan cheese, shredded
Salt and freshly ground pepper to taste
Olive oil as needed

Heat oven to 400°F. In medium bowl, combine asparagus, tomatoes, mushrooms, artichokes, marinade.

Mix together flour, yogurt, baking powder, 1 teaspoon salt, paprika, oregano, chili powder. Cover a half sheet pan with olive oil, flatten out the dough to fill pan. Flip once, sprinkle a bit of mozzarella, bake for 5 minutes. Top with veg in layer from edge to edge of dough, top with rest of mozzarella, bake 10 more minutes. Drizzle with olive oil, sprinkle with ⅔ of Parmesan, bake another 5 minutes.

Top with remaining Parmesan, garnish with a few grinds of freshly ground pepper, cut, serve.

Garden of Eden Vegetable Soup

Makes 6 to 8 servings

- 2 tablespoons olive oil
- 1 medium red onion, diced
- 4 cups celery, sliced thin
- 1 medium Granny Smith apple, peeled, cored, and chopped
- 1 tablespoon chili powder
- ½ teaspoon ground cumin
- 4 cups vegetable broth (broths have salt; I've omitted salt from the recipe, add if you prefer)
- 1 medium zucchini, chopped
- 3 cups cauliflower florets, in bite-size pieces
- 4 cups kale, chopped and packed
- ½ teaspoon freshly ground pepper

To large pot or Dutch oven, over medium-high heat, add onion, celery, apple. Cook, stirring, till onions are translucent, about 4 minutes. Stir in chili powder and cumin.

Add kale, stirring till wilted, about 3 minutes. Add zucchini, cauliflower, broth, pepper. Bring to a boil, reduce heat to a simmer, cover and cook till vegetables are very tender, 35 minutes.

Taste for seasoning, adding salt or pepper if needed. Serve hot.

Green Goddess Tossed Salad

Makes 4 to 6 servings

An old school Americana salad dressing favorite. Almost so good you don't need the salad. Butter lettuce and slices of colorful bell pepper go well with this dressing.

- ¾ cup mayonnaise
- ⅓ cup sour cream
- 3 scallions, white and green parts, sliced thin (about ½ cup)
- 3 tablespoons chopped fresh chives
- ¼ cup fresh tarragon leaves, chopped fine (about 1 tablespoon)
- 1 clove garlic, minced
- 3 anchovy fillets, minced
- 1 ½ tablespoons fresh lemon juice
- 1 tablespoon coarsely ground pepper
- 1 teaspoon hot sauce

Combine all ingredients in medium bowl, stir together vigorously.

Cover and refrigerate for 2 hours before serving over a bounteous green salad.

Roasted Carrots and Radishes with Spring Vinaigrette

Makes 6 servings

- 3 tablespoons red wine vinegar
- 1 clove garlic, crushed
- 5 tablespoons olive oil, divided
- 2 pounds small rainbow carrots, about 18
- 1 bunch large radishes, about 8
- 2 tablespoons fresh thyme leaves
- Salt and freshly ground pepper

In small bowl or measuring cup, combine vinegar, garlic, ¼ teaspoon each salt and pepper. While whisking, slowly add 3 tablespoons oil. Let mixture "find itself" for about 20 minutes in fridge. Remove garlic.

Heat oven to 450°F. Wash and peel carrots, trim ends, cut in half lengthwise. Wash radishes, trim ends, halve lengthwise.

On a baking sheet, place vegetables, drizzle with 2 tablespoons olive oil, rub to coat the vegetables. Sprinkle with thyme leaves, salt and pepper.

Roast for 20 to 25 minutes till tender when pierced with knife.

Drizzle with dressing, serve immediately.

Brown Sugar Creole Mustard Jalapeño Ham

Makes 12 servings

New Orleans meets Texas in this sassy spicy ham.

- 1 fully cooked butt portion bone-in half ham, 8 to 9 pounds
- 1 cup dark brown sugar, packed
- ½ cup Creole or spicy coarse-grained mustard
- 2 tablespoons finely minced pickled jalapeño peppers
- ¼ cup honey
- 1 cup orange juice

Unwrap him, er, ham, bring to room temperature for one hour.

For glaze, in small pot, combine sugar, mustard, jalapeño, honey, orange juice. Bring to a simmer over medium heat and cook till reduced by half, 30 minutes. Glaze should look shiny and slightly thickened.

Heat oven to 325°F. Place rack in roasting pan, set ham on rack, fat side up. Fill pan with ½ to ¾ inches of water. Cover tightly with foil and bake for 2 hours 15 minutes for a 9-pound ham. 10 minutes less for an 8-pound.

Thirty minutes before ham finishes baking, uncover and increase oven temperature to 400°F. During this last 30 minutes, brush ham generously with glaze every 10 minutes. At the end of this process ham should be gloriously caramelized and have an internal temperature of at least 130°F. Remove from oven and let rest uncovered at least 15 minutes before carving. Internal temperature should rise about 10 degrees as it rests.

Crabby McCrab Cakes with By the Sea Tartar Coulis

(Try saying that three times fast)

CRAB CAKES

Makes 6 cakes. Next to no filler, more yummy crab.

- 5 tablespoons mayonnaise
- 1 large egg, beaten
- 2 teaspoons Worcestershire sauce
- 1 teaspoons Creole or spicy coarse-grained mustard
- 1 ½ teaspoons Old Bay seasoning
- ½ teaspoon salt
- ½ cup scallions, green parts and a bit of white, sliced thin
- ¼ cup chopped parsley
- ¼ cup finely chopped red bell pepper
- 1 pound jumbo lump crab meat, cleaned
- ¾ cup panko breadcrumbs
- Butter, for greasing the baking sheet
- Lemon wedges for serving

To a large bowl, add mayo, egg, Worcestershire, mustard, Old Bay, salt, whisk to combine. Add parsley, scallions, bell pepper, crab meat, panko crumbs. Fold all together thoroughly but gently so as not to damage the crab. Cover and refrigerate 3 hours, to overnight.

Heat oven to 450°F. Very thoroughly butter a half sheet pan or baking sheet. Divide crab mixture into 6 portions and shape into individual patties, set on the pan. They should be like pincushions not like pancakes. Bake for 13 minutes till lightly browned. Using flat spatula, remove from baking sheet to plate carefully. They will still seem a bit loosely assembled. This is a good thing. Serve immediately with plenty of lemon wedges and tartar coulis!

TARTAR COULIS

Makes 6 servings

- ¾ cup mayonnaise
- 1 teaspoon capers, drained
- ½ teaspoon red wine vinegar
- 1 teaspoon lemon juice
- 1 teaspoon Creole or spicy coarse-grained mustard
- ⅓ cup kosher dill pickles
- ½ small red onion, chopped coarse
- ⅓ cup Italian parsley
- 1 heaping tablespoon sliced pickled jalapeño peppers
- 3 tablespoons fresh tarragon leaves

In small bowl, combine mayo, capers, vinegar, lemon juice, mustard. In food processor, combine pickle, onion, parsley, jalapeño, tarragon. Pulse till chunky or fine as desired. Strain pickle mixture of liquid, then add to mayo mixture and stir thoroughly. Cover and chill in fridge for 2 hours before serving. Even better the next day!

Pro Tip: You'll LOVE this sauce, but my crab cakes are so flavorful, you might decide to use it on something more plain, and that's okay!

Salmon Patsy

Makes 2 servings

You've heard of Bananas Foster, Fettuccine Alfredo and Steak Diane . . . I now proudly present: Salmon Patsy! A humble topping of garlic, lemon and Parmesan takes this dish to such an absolutely fabulous level it's practically immoral.

- 3 tablespoons extra virgin olive oil
- 3 tablespoons grated Parmesan cheese
- Juice of 1 lemon
- 3 tablespoons fresh parsley, chopped fine
- 1 tablespoon dehydrated Cajun or Creole Trinity seasoning (celery, bell pepper, onion)
- 1 tablespoon garlic, minced
- 2 twelve-ounce salmon fillets
- Coarse salt
- 1 tablespoon coarsely ground fresh pepper

Heat oven to 375°F.

Mix together olive oil, cheese, lemon juice, parsley, Cajun seasoning and garlic. You can easily double the measurements if preparing four fillets. Be casual about it, the amounts don't need to be exact.

Salt and pepper the fillets and place them skin down on a foil-covered baking sheet or pan. Bake for 18 minutes. Remove from oven and spoon the Parmesan-parsley mixture evenly over the top of each fillet.

Return to oven and bake for 5 minutes. Heat broiler. Broil fillets for additional 4 minutes. Watch carefully! A bit of blackening of the garlic is desirable. Charred smoking ruins is not the look you're going for. Ovens do differ.

With spatula, separate fillet from its skin (leaving skin behind). Serve with brown rice, a salad, and festive green vegetable!

NATIONAL EAT YOUR VEGETABLES DAY: JUNE 17

BROCCOLI
COLLARD GREENS
KALE
ROMAINE LETTUCE
SPINACH
ARTICHOKES
ASPARAGUS
BEETS
BRUSSELS SPROUTS
CABBAGE
CAULIFLOWER
CELERY
CUCUMBERS
EGGPLANT
GREEN BEANS
MUSHROOMS
OKRA
ONIONS
ZUCCHINI
SWEET POTATO
BUTTERNUT SQUASH
CARROTS
BELL PEPPERS
BOK CHOY

Hot Cross Buns
Makes 18 buns

The Good Friday custom. "Get them while they're hot, eat them by the ton. One a penny, two a penny, hot cross buns."

⅓ cup unsalted butter, melted, plus more for greasing

2 large eggs, room temperature

1 teaspoon vanilla extract

4 cups unbleached all-purpose flour

1 teaspoon ground cardamom

½ teaspoon ground nutmeg

½ cup dried currants

1 tablespoon grated orange zest

1 large egg yolk

2 cups confectioners' sugar

½ teaspoon orange extract

2 tablespoons, plus 2 teaspoons whole milk

½ cup sugar, plus a pinch, divided

2 (¼-ounce) packets active dry yeast

1 cup whole milk

In small, not clear, bowl, combine a pinch of sugar and ⅓ cup very warm water. (Very warm water is the temperature you'd feel comfortable taking a shower in if you hold your finger under the tap to test, 103°F to 105°F.) Add the yeast to the sugar water, stir to dissolve completely. Cover bowl with dark cloth or plate and set aside till foamy, 7 minutes. Heat milk in medium pot over medium-high heat till bubbles form around edge, about 2 minutes. In large bowl, combine warm milk, yeast mixture, sugar, butter, whole eggs, vanilla extract, whisk together thoroughly.

In another bowl, whisk flour, cardamom, and nutmeg together. With wooden spoon, gradually add flour mixture to large bowl, stirring into wet ingredients till dough begins to form.

Add orange zest, knead in bowl to combine. Turn soft and sticky dough out onto lightly floured surface and knead till elastic and still sticky, least 8 minutes. Lastly, add and knead the currants into dough.

Generously butter the inside of a large bowl, add dough, turn to coat with butter. Cover bowl tightly with plastic wrap, then a dark towel, and place in a warm spot to rise. Dough should double in size in about 1 ½ hours.

Grease a 9 x 13-inch baking dish with unsalted butter. Lightly butter your hands. Form 18 balls 2 inches in size and place next to each other in dish.

Whisk together the egg yolk with 1 teaspoon water, brush tops of buns. Cover with a towel and let rise in warm place till doubled in size, about 45 minutes.

Heat oven to 375°F. Bake for 20 minutes till golden brown.

Cool buns in pan for at least 10 minutes. Meanwhile, in large bowl combine confectioners' sugar, orange extract, and milk, using large spoon to stir well. The icing should be thick but pipe-able. Using a pastry bag with tip, or plastic storage bag with tiny corner cut off, pipe a cross shape on top of buns. When icing has hardened, about 10 minutes, cut buns apart gently with a bread knife, and serve.

½ cup
Numbers 17:8
And it came to pass, that on the morrow Moses went into the tabernacle of witness; and, behold, the rod of Aaron for the house of Levi was budded, and brought forth buds, and bloomed blossoms, and yielded almonds.

2 cups
Jeremiah 6:20
To what purpose cometh there to me incense from Sheba, and the sweet cane from a far country? Your burnt offerings are not acceptable, nor your sacrifices sweet unto me.

1 ¼ cups
Judges 5:25
He asked for water, and she gave him milk; she brought forth *butter* in a lordly dish.

5 large
Isaiah 10:14
And my hand hath found as a nest the riches of the people: and as one gathereth eggs that are left, have I gathered all the earth; and there was none that moved the wing, or opened the mouth, or peeped.

2 ½ cups
1 Kings 4:22
And Solomon's provision for one day was thirty measures of fine flour, and threescore measures of meal . . .

2 tablespoons
1 Samuel 14:25
And all they of the land came to a wood; and there was honey upon the ground.

½ teaspoon
Mark 9:50
Salt is good: but if the salt have lost his saltness, where-with will ye season it? Have salt in yourselves, and have peace with another.

1 ¾ total teaspoons
1 Kings 10:10
And she gave the king an hundred and twenty talents of gold, and of spices very great store, and precious stones: there came no more such abundance of spices as these which the queen of Sheba gave to King Solomon.

5 total teaspoons
1 Corinthians 5:6
Your glorying is not good. Know ye not that a little leaven leaveneth the whole lump?

7 ounces
Song of Solomon 2:13
The fig tree putteth forth her green figs, and the vines with the tender grape give a good smell. Arise, my love, my fair one, and come away.

¾ cup
1 Samuel 30:12
And they gave him a piece of a cake of figs, and two clusters of raisins; and when he had eaten, his spirit came again to him; for he had eaten no bread, nor drunk any water, three days and three nights.

¾ cup
1 Corinthians 9:7
Who goeth a warfare any time at his own charges? Who planteth a vineyard, and eateth not of the fruit thereof? Or who feedeth a flock, and eateth not of the milk of the flock?

Scripture Cake

Q: What book in the New Testament says men must make the coffee? A: He-brews. Seriously folks, the Scripture Cake has been around a long time. The idea is to test your knowledge of your bible verses by giving you a measure (½ cup) and a verse (Numbers 17:8). It's up to you to know that means almonds. I've helped you by writing it out like you're used to seeing a recipe, below. It's really yummy too.

½ cup sliced almonds

2 cups light brown sugar, packed

1 ¼ cups (2 ½ sticks) salted butter, plus more to grease pan

2 tablespoons honey

5 large eggs

2 ½ cups unbleached all-purpose flour, plus more to flour pan

2 teaspoons baking powder

1 teaspoon baking soda

2 teaspoons cornstarch

½ teaspoon salt

1 teaspoon ground cinnamon

½ teaspoon ground nutmeg

¼ teaspoon ground ginger

7 ounces sundried figs, remove stems, chop

¾ cup raisins

¾ cup whole milk

Heat oven to 325°F. Toast almonds on cookie sheet till slightly browned, about 7 minutes. Grease and flour 10-inch Bundt pan. In medium bowl, cream together sugar, butter, honey. Add eggs one at a time, incorporate well. In second bowl whisk together flour, baking powder, baking soda, cornstarch, salt, cinnamon, nutmeg, ginger. In third bowl combine almonds, figs, raisins, toss with some flour till coated. Add fruit mixture to bowl with butter-eggs, mix well. Add remaining flour in three stages, incorporating thoroughly with a wooden spoon. Add milk, stir. Pour batter into prepared pan. Bake for 60 minutes. Make sure a toothpick comes out clean and you're done. Cool 5 minutes in pan before turning out.

April Showers and One to Grow On

Cucumber Sandwiches

Makes about 70 canapés

Let's start this chapter about tea parties, showers, and birthdays off with a fitting treat. An English teatime tradition, perfected by my dear Grandma Hittie as her signature party appetizer during a storied career as hostess in Houston, Texas. The following sticks closely by her recipe, with two flourishes, one from the country, one from the city. Can you guess? The hot sauce and the dill garnish, 'a course.

1 loaf (1 pound) premium white sandwich bread, unwrapped, stacked on one end, overnight. Lock up your ducks and goats so they can't get at it.

1 package (8 ounces) package cream cheese, softened to room temperature

¾ cup high quality mayonnaise

1 tablespoon fresh lemon juice

1 tablespoon your favorite hot sauce

2 teaspoons Worcestershire sauce

1 teaspoon Lawry's Seasoned Salt, or to taste

1 hothouse (English) cucumber, peeled, seeded, and grated (about ½ cup)

1 small onion, finely grated (¼ cup)

1 hothouse cucumber, scored with a sharp-tined fork lengthwise to create a scalloped edge when sliced. Then sliced very thin crosswise with a sharp knife.

Fresh dill, to garnish 70 canapés

In a medium bowl, mix together cream cheese, mayo, lemon juice, Worcestershire, hot sauce, seasoned salt, grated cucumber, grated onion. Refrigerate spread for at least 2 hours, even overnight, as Grandma says, "so the seasoning goes through well!"

Cut crusts from bread and cut each slice into four pieces. Spread each piece thinly with 1 teaspoon cream cheese mixture, then top with a slice of cucumber. Refrigerate between sheets of wax paper or parchment for at least an hour before serving. Will keep for up to 24 hours in advance of party. Before serving, top each with a sprig of dill to garnish.

BRIDAL SHOWER

A bridal shower is for the bride, a wedding shower includes the groom. Friends and family should plan, invite, and host. There are so many great themes, like a "stock the kitchen" gift shower, a shower that celebrates the future locale of their destination wedding, a shower that's all about their favorite sports team. And people love games. How well do you know the bride and groom? Print up a quiz with questions like "Where was their first date?"; "Who's his favorite singer?"; "What color are her eyes?" and see who gets the most answers right!

Pimento Cheese Saint Peter

Makes 24 servings

This southern American party classic gets a kick from dill pickle and the heat of a little jalapeño. Named for the street of my former apartment in the French Quarter, in which Tennessee Williams wrote A Streetcar Named Desire.

½ cup kosher dill pickles

2 tablespoons pickled jalapeño peppers, drained

16 ounces extra sharp Cracker Barrel cheddar, shredded with grater or food processor

½ cup Parmesan cheese, shredded

½ cup mayonnaise

2 jars (4 ounces) diced pimentos, drained

1 heaping tablespoon dehydrated Cajun or Creole Trinity (celery, bell pepper, onion)

1 teaspoon coarsely ground fresh pepper

In food processor, add pickles, jalapeños, pulse till chopped fine. To large bowl, add cheddar, Parmesan, mayo, pickles, jalapeños, pimentos, dehydrated trinity, pepper. Thoroughly combine with wooden spoon. Chill covered for 6 hours, or overnight, before serving with bell pepper, celery sticks, carrots, and crackers. Makes enough for two 12-person parties!

Deviled Ham Canapés

Makes 40 canapés

- 1 pound sliced or cubed ham
- 4 ounces cream cheese, softened
- ½ cup mayonnaise
- ¼ cup pickle relish
- 1 tablespoon dried parsley flakes
- 1 tablespoon smoked paprika
- 2 teaspoons yellow mustard
- 1 teaspoon onion powder
- Couple dashes hot sauce
- Ritz crackers
- About 15 cornichons for garnish
- Diced pimento for garnish (optional)

BABY Shower

Combine ham, cream cheese, mayo, relish, parsley flakes, paprika, mustard, onion powder, hot sauce. In food processor, pulse till spreadable. Pipe or spread deviled ham on crackers. Slice cornichons and garnish each canapé with a piece or two, accompanied by a pinch of pimento.

This shower is really for mom. Friends, family, and even baby's dad can be in charge of hosting this one. Grandmas-to-be should get a lot of input. (You're welcome.) Anywhere from seven months pregnant to post-delivery can be a preferred time for one of these shindigs. Ask the mom and dad-to-be what time they'd like best. Make sure to coordinate guest gifts so there aren't a lot of duplicates. Mini plastic babies (like king cake babies) scattered everywhere are a festive decoration. (Make sure there aren't any toddlers or pets who might swallow them!) If you're into gender revealing, this could be that party too. If not, it's just as much fun to have a pink and blue party!

Ambrosia Salad

Makes 8 servings

A traditional, and ambrosial, shower party classic.

1 ½ cups green grapes

1 can (11 ounces) mandarin oranges, drained

1 jar (10 ounces) maraschino cherries, drained and patted dry

1 can (20 ounces) pineapple chunks, drained

½ teaspoon grated lemon zest

1 cup heavy cream, beaten to stiff peaks

1 tablespoon sugar

½ cup mayonnaise

1 cup mini marshmallows

In medium bowl, combine grapes, oranges, cherries, pineapple.

In large bowl, combine sugar, mayo, lemon zest. Stir to dissolve sugar. Fold in whipped cream, marshmallows. With slotted spoon, add fruit, fold just to combine.

Transfer to 2-quart dish, freeze for 1 hour before serving.

WEDDING

Anniversary Themes

1	Paper
2	Cotton
3	Leather
4	Fruit, Flowers
5	Wood
6	Iron
7	Copper
8	Bronze
9	Pottery
10	Tin
15	Crystal
20	China
25	Silver
30	Pearl
35	Coral
40	Ruby
45	Sapphire
50	Gold
55	Emerald
60	Diamond

Queen for a Day Drop Scones

Makes 16 scones

Long live the scones. My recipe follows Queen Elizabeth II's original 1959 method and ingredients closely. She famously cooked them for Eisenhower at Balmoral then mailed him the recipe as a souvenir. I halved it, to suit the more casual get-togethers you might plan when outside the castle.

- **1 large egg**
- **¼ cup sugar**
- **¾ cup whole milk**
- **1 ½ cups unbleached all-purpose flour**
- **1 ½ teaspoons cream of tartar**
- **1 ½ teaspoons baking powder**
- **2 tablespoons unsalted butter, melted**
- **5 teaspoons canola oil, divided**

In large bowl, stir together eggs, sugar, and half the milk. In second bowl, whisk together flour, baking powder, cream of tartar. Slowly add flour mixture to wet mixture, stirring in thoroughly with wooden spoon. Add rest of milk as desired to get preferred batter consistency. Then mix in butter.

Heat a cast iron pan or griddle over medium heat, add 2 teaspoons oil to cook first batch of scones, 1 teaspoon for each batch following.

When oil is hot, drop a heaping tablespoon of batter for each scone into the pan. When browned on bottom, about three minutes, turn and cook another two minutes till brown. Serve with syrup and strawberries. Butter and raspberry jam to accompany are also scrummy.

HOW TO POACH an EGG

Fill a medium pot with water and two tablespoons vinegar to help set the whites of the eggs. Bring water to a simmer. While waiting for the water, add one egg to a small bowl or ramekin. Stir the simmering water gently in a circle. Slide egg into center of whirlpool, let it spin as the water slows. The white should wrap itself around the yolk. Cook for 3 minutes, remove egg with slotted spoon to bowl of cool water, then dry on paper towel. Repeat till all eggs are done.

Princess Diana's B.J.P.'s
Baked Jacket Potatoes

Makes 4 B.J.P.'s

I created this recipe after viewing Royal Chef Graham Newbould's demo of The Princess of Wales' favorite B.J.P.'s in the video special Secrets of the Royal Kitchen. *He says to enjoy with a nice avocado salad.*

4 medium baking potatoes

4 large eggs, poached soft

3 tablespoons salted butter, softened, plus
    2 tablespoons

2 tablespoons all-purpose flour

1 ¾ cups whole milk, divided

4 ounces Gruyère cheese, shredded

1 pound peeled tail-off shrimp, cooked and
    halved crosswise

¼ cup grated Parmesan cheese

Salt and ground white pepper

Heat oven to 350°F. Pierce each potato several times with a fork and bake for 60 to 70 minutes, or till knife easily pierces, set aside. Meanwhile, poach your eggs softly (see prior page), set aside. Slice top third off potatoes and scoop flesh out. In mixing bowl mash briefly with 3 tablespoons of softened butter, ¼ cup milk, ½ teaspoon salt. Add a bit more milk if needed to make sure they will pipe well. Place mashed potatoes in piping bag with a large open star pastry tip.

In medium saucepan over medium heat melt 2 tablespoons butter. Add flour, cook for two minutes whisking constantly. Slowly add 1 ½ cups milk while whisking, bring just to a boil. Reduce heat and simmer gently 5 minutes, stirring occasionally till thickened. Add cheese and stir till melted. Mix in shrimp. Add ⅛ teaspoon white pepper and salt to taste. Fill potato jackets half full with cheese and shrimp mixture, reserving some sauce. Set poached egg on top. Pipe mashed potatoes with a zig-zag motion around rim of filled potato, leaving egg in center exposed. Spoon a bit of cheese sauce over egg, sprinkle on Parmesan. In a 375°F oven, on a sheet pan, bake the four B.J.P.'s for 10 minutes. Next, run under broiler till edges of piped potato have browned slightly, 2 to 3 minutes.

Malibu Hummus

Makes 24 servings

The Middle East goes Hollywood with this healthy partner to crudités and crackers. Cannellini beans, sundried tomatoes, and an array of Southwestern seasonings will set off searchlights in the sky at your next festive get-together. And the winner is . . . Malibu Hummus!

1 clove garlic

1 small red onion, quartered

⅓ cup drained marinated sundried tomatoes

½ cup Italian parsley, loosely packed

1 can (15.5 ounces) cannellini beans, drained

1 can (15.5 ounces) garbanzo beans, drained

2 tablespoons canola oil

2 tablespoons prepared horseradish

1 tablespoon Tabasco green pepper sauce

1 tablespoon freshly ground pepper

1 teaspoons ground cumin

1 teaspoon chili powder

Juice of 2 limes

½ cup (4 ounces) sour cream

Pro Tip: for your next Oscars party menu, this is an ideal munchie snack if you're looking for one.

In bowl of food processor combine garlic, onion, sundried tomatoes, parsley, pulse till finely chopped, do not purée. Transfer to medum mixing bowl. In processor, combine the beans, oil, horseradish, Tabasco, black pepper, cumin, chili powder, lime juice. Process till smooth. Add bean mixture to sundried tomato mixture. Mix in sour cream. Refrigerate hummus for at least 1 hour to let flavors meld.

NATIONAL EAT WHAT
YOU WANT DAY:
MAY 11

Happy Birthday Hamburger Sliders   *Makes 12 sliders*

2 pounds ground chuck (80% lean)

2 tablespoons Creole or spicy coarse-grained mustard

1 small sweet onion, chopped fine, about ½ cup

3 tablespoons finely chopped parsley

¼ cup panko breadcrumbs

1 teaspoon salt

½ teaspoon freshly ground pepper

1 tablespoon olive oil

12 slices extra sharp cheddar cheese

12 red onions slices

12 tomato slices

Romaine lettuce, chopped

12 slider buns or sandwich-size rolls, lightly toasted

Pickle relish, mayonnaise, ketchup

In large bowl, mix together ground chuck, mustard, onion, parsley, panko, salt, pepper. Form 12 cute 'n chubby patties about 2 ½-inches wide each.

In a large cast iron pan (preferable) or large skillet, heat the oil over medium-high heat.

Cook each patty, turning at least once, about 8 minutes total or till done as desired. During last minute of cooking place cheese atop each burger as desired, cover pan about 30 seconds to melt cheese slightly.

Serve on toasted buns with toppings and condiments.

World's Most Delicious Three-Layer White Cake

"A party without a cake is just a meeting."
— *Julia Child*

3 cups unbleached all-purpose flour, more for pans

2 cups sugar

1 tablespoon and ½ teaspoon baking powder

1 teaspoon salt

1 cup (2 sticks) unsalted butter, softened, more for pans

2 large eggs, 4 large egg whites

1 cup whole milk

2 teaspoons vanilla extract

Heat oven to 350°F. Generously grease and flour three 8-inch cake pans.

In large bowl, whisk together flour, sugar, baking powder, salt. Using your hands, add butter to dry ingredients, work together till sandy in texture. With electric mixer, on slow speed, add each whole egg and egg white, one at a time. Batter may be lumpy to start with. In small bowl, combine milk and vanilla extract. With mixer on medium, add milk mixture to batter in two additions, combining completely.

With large spoon, divide batter evenly among three pans. Shake each pan side to side to even batter out. Bake, rotating pans from front to back once, till a toothpick comes out clean, about 35 minutes. Don't undercook. Cool completely, then frost! (See end of this chapter for frosting recipes.)

The Fortune Cake

Makes 8 servings

A word to the host: when your guests choose their slice of the Fortune Cake and hear their "fate," they might interpret it a little more meaningfully than you expect. Remind them it's just a game. Can be played with less than eight, or more. Have more than one guest choose the same numbered slice and they can share the fortune (and the cake).

3 cups all-purpose flour, plus more for flouring pans

2 cups sugar

1 tablespoon and ½ teaspoon baking powder

1 teaspoon salt

1 cup (2 sticks) unsalted butter, softened, and more for pans

4 large egg whites, 2 large whole eggs

1 cup milk

2 teaspoons vanilla extract

8 colors gel food coloring: red; orange; yellow; royal blue; shamrock green; violet; aqua (or turquoise); and pink
NOTE: common food color will not work well for this.

12 ounces orange marmalade (the kind with sugar)

1 tube yellow or white decorating gel

Sanding sugar, two colors of your choice (optional)

Heat oven to 350°F. Generously grease and flour four 4 x 8-inch loaf pans. Bake the cake layers in two batches, no more, or uncooked batter will begin to set.

In a large bowl, whisk together flour, sugar, baking powder, salt. Using your hands, add butter to dry ingredients till sandy in texture. With electric mixer, on slow speed, add each white and whole egg one at a time, mixing in thoroughly. Don't worry if batter is lumpy to start with. In a small bowl, stir together milk and vanilla extract. With mixer on medium speed, add milk mixture to the batter in two additions, combining completely.

Divide batter ¾ cup each between 8 bowls, stir in a few drops of each gel color to shade desired. Place batter in prepared pans one at a time, shake or tap each pan side to side to flatten batter out. Bake on center rack, rotating once, till a toothpick comes out clean, about 17 minutes per batch. Don't undercook. Cool completely. In a very clean 4 x 8-inch loaf pan, place the first of the eight layers of cake. Being as random as you prefer, but perhaps alternating colors that are least alike, begin horizontally stacking the rest of the layers on top of the first, spreading a generous amount of orange marmalade between each layer. Do not put marmalade on the final top layer. The stack will be a couple of inches in height above the edge of the loaf pan. *(Continued)*

THE FORTUNE CAKE

1 YOU WILL FIND LOVE

2 A WISH YOU HOLD SINCERELY WILL COME TRUE

3 YOU WILL CHANGE DIRECTION

4 YOU WILL MEET AN EXTRAORDINARY FRIEND

5 YOU WILL MAKE AN IMPORTANT JOURNEY

6 SOMETHING WILL COME TO AN END

7 YOU WILL LEARN A POWERFUL LESSON

8 KARMA WILL FIND YOU, MAY IT BE A BLESSING

Chocolate Frosting

(For a 3-layer cake, double the recipe)

- 1 cup (2 sticks) unsalted butter, room temperature
- ½ cup Dutch processed cocoa powder
- 4 cups confectioners' sugar
- ½ teaspoon salt
- 2 to 3 tablespoons milk, more as needed

In large bowl using electric mixer on low speed combine butter, cocoa powder. Blend in sugar a cup or so at a time, salt, and milk till smooth and creamy.

The Fortune Cake, continued.

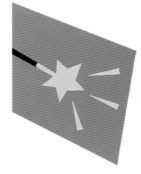

Next, pack a 3-inch layer of paper toweling in the bottom of a second loaf pan, then invert on top of the stack of cake layers, pressing them down and in effect making a "closed box" of the two pans. Secure with heavy tape then tightly enclose in plastic wrap. Refrigerate overnight.

Next day, remove Fortune Cake from its "box." Lay on serving plate so layers are perpendicular to plate (as shown above). Make chocolate frosting (recipe in sidebar). Frost, keeping track of where the dividing line of each layer roughly is. Pipe a line of decorating gel to mark each dividing line, decorate cake with sanding sugar. If you have other festoons to adorn the top of cake, add these now.

At serving time, decide which way you will count the layers (normally left to right, making sure your cuts will align with how the layers lie under the frosting). Ask each guest to pick a number from 1 to 8. Cut the cake, keeping close track of which number relates to which slice. Even if you cut the slices with a bit of irregularity so you pick up some of another layer, in the main it should be clear which color you're cutting. Next, consult the picture on the prior page to determine everyone's fortunes!

Cream Cheese Frosting

(For a 3-layer cake, double recipe. Tint pink and add princess-themed toppers for a princess cake!)

>   5 tablespoons butter, room temperature
>
>   8 ounces cream cheese, room temperature
>
>   5 cups confectioners' sugar
>
>   1 teaspoon vanilla extract
>
>   1 tablespoon whole milk, more as required

In large bowl, with electric mixer, beat together butter and cream cheese till combined. Add confectioners' sugar, ½ cup at a time, beating after each addition. Add vanilla. Add milk. Should be stiffly smooth.

Peanut Butter Frosting

(For a 3-layer cake, double recipe)

>   1 cup (2 sticks) unsalted butter, room temperature
>
>   1 cup creamy peanut butter (I use Skippy)
>
>   3 cups confectioners' sugar
>
>   1 teaspoon vanilla extract
>
>   ½ teaspoon salt
>
>   3 tablespoons milk, more as needed

In a large bowl, with electric mixer, beat together butter and peanut butter. Add sugar a bit at a time till combined. Add vanilla, salt, milk, mix till smooth.

MUSIC TO PARTY* BY

Today there are more ways than ever to have rapturous custom tunage for your bountiful brunches and chic soirées. My favorite way is to create my own mixes (inspired by occasion and theme) using tracks from my iTunes library.

With a program called djay Pro, I mix the songs together into longer medley tracks (with simple but cool custom transitions between songs) then organize them on my iPad. I then use strategically-placed bluetooth speakers to bless every heart with the sound of music. Or, you could just use your fave online streaming service, or even pull out your old vinyl LPs and stereophonic player. Let's get harmonied up!

* and cook

Seven Songs FOR SINGING

WE'LL TAKE A CUP
OF KINDNESS YET
FOR
AULD
LANG
SYNE

Original arrangements by Tim Denbo

The Yankee Doodle Boy

I'm a Yan-kee Doo-dle Dan - dy, A Yan-kee Doo-dle, do or die;___ A real live

nep-hew of my Un-cle Sam, Born on the Fourth of Ju - ly.___ I've got a

Yan-kee Doo-dle sweet - heart, She's my Yan-kee Doo-dle joy.___ Yan-kee Doo-dle

came to Lon-don, just to ride the po - nies; I am the Yan-kee Doo-dle Boy.___

The Eyes Of Texas

Amazing Grace

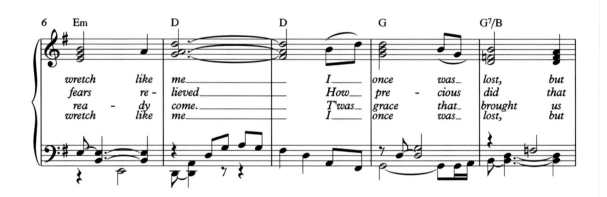

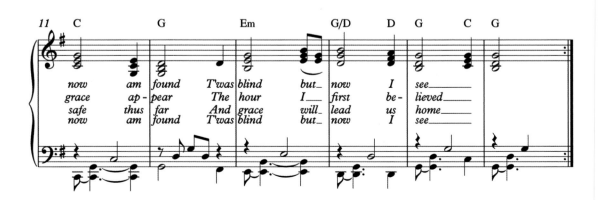

Here We Come A-Caroling

Away In A Manger

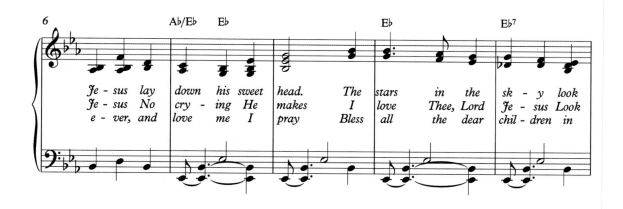

Aloha 'Oe
(Farewell To Thee)

Auld Lang Syne

Summer
Solstice

My Little Grass Shack: A Polynesian Luau

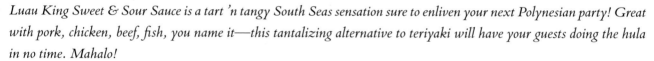

Cocktail Franks with Luau King Sweet & Sour Sauce

Makes 60 franks and about 2 cups sauce

Luau King Sweet & Sour Sauce is a tart 'n tangy South Seas sensation sure to enliven your next Polynesian party! Great with pork, chicken, beef, fish, you name it—this tantalizing alternative to teriyaki will have your guests doing the hula in no time. Mahalo!

1 cup sweetened applesauce

½ cup duck sauce

¼ cup chili sauce

2 teaspoons prepared horseradish, drained

2 teaspoons apple cider vinegar

1 teaspoon fresh lemon juice

1 teaspoon coarsely ground pepper

60 cocktail franks

In a small bowl, stir together all ingredients except franks. Refrigerate Luau King Sauce for at least 2 hours before using. In a large skillet over medium-high heat, add about ¼ cup water and cook cocktail franks, turning a few times till plump and heated-through, about 3 minutes. Drain and keep warm. When it's party time, serve franks with toothpicks and sauce. Rock-a-hula baby!

The Tiki Man

Makes 2 servings

That Tiki Man has a tasty way about him.

¼ cup plus 2 tablespoons soy sauce, divided
1 tablespoon apple cider vinegar
2 teaspoons sugar
1 teaspoon ground ginger
2 cloves garlic, minced
2 large, boneless skinless chicken breasts
¼ cup peanut oil
¼ cup all-purpose flour
Salt and freshly ground pepper
2 large eggs, lightly beaten
1 cup finely chopped macadamia nuts
One 8-ounce, or larger, boneless ham steak
24-30 whole cloves
8 canned mandarin orange segments
1 large grape tomato
1 scallion, green part only, cut into four 2-inch lengths

In medium bowl, stir together ¼ cup soy sauce, vinegar, sugar, ginger, garlic. Marinate chicken breasts in mixture for 30 minutes.

Heat oven to 375°F.

In a medium skillet, heat peanut oil over low heat. Arrange three plates for dredging breasts: the first with flour, salt, and pepper, the second with the egg, the third with nuts. Drain breasts and pat dry. Dredge breasts in flour, dip in egg, roll in nuts. Increase heat to medium-high and fry about 6 minutes per side till dark golden brown. Transfer to a parchment-lined sheet pan or greased oven-safe dish, bake 15 minutes more. Reduce oven to 275°F.

Cut two slices of ham into classic Tiki Man mouth shape (see photo). Cut a large grape tomato crosswise.

On each nut-crusted chicken breast, place a ham mouth studded with 24-30 clove teeth each (upper and lower), a grape tomato nose, two mandarin orange eyes with two segments each forming almond shapes. Affix mouths with toothpicks as needed. Place in 275°F oven for 8 minutes. Serve.

SPAM Fantasia Skewers

Makes 10 skewers

American troops brought SPAM to Hawaii during World War II and it took Polynesia by storm. I call these Fantasia Skewers because they're so fantastically zesty and zany.

1 can (12 ounces) SPAM, cut in about 24 cubes
3 cans (8 ounces each) pineapple chunks
Ten 8-inch wood skewers, soaked in water for 5 minutes
½ cup teriyaki sauce

Heat oven broiler. Alternate cubes of SPAM and pineapple on wood skewers so there are 5 or 6 total cubes on each, lay on sheet pan or cookie sheet, brush generously with teriyaki on all sides.

On center oven rack, broil 3 to 4 minutes on one side, watching carefully to keep from burning. Turn once, broil another 2 to 3 minutes. Broilers and times may vary. On a festive plate or platter, serve while warm.

Loco Moco

Makes 4 servings

The classic Hawaiian plate lunch.

4 cups boil-in-bag rice (2 packages)

¾ pound lean ground beef

⅔ cup panko breadcrumbs

1 large egg, lightly beaten

1 medium onion, minced, divided

2 tablespoons Worcestershire sauce, divided

Couple of dashes of your favorite hot sauce

1 ½ teaspoons salt, divided

2 tablespoons olive oil, divided

4 large eggs

2 tablespoons butter, divided

2 tablespoons flour

1 cup beef broth

4 or 5 scallions, green parts, thinly sliced on an
angle, divided

Heat oven to 200°F.

Cook rice per package instructions, set aside.

In medium bowl, mix together beef, breadcrumbs, egg, half the minced onion, 1 tablespoon Worcestershire, hot sauce, and salt. Form meat into four 4-inch patties, set aside.

In large skillet, heat 1 tablespoon olive oil and fry four eggs sunny-side up with white fully set. Sprinkle with salt. Place on an oven-safe plate or pan on wet paper towels and hold in the warm oven for later.

Wipe out skillet and over medium-high heat, cook hamburger patties till brown and crusty outside, medium rare inside, adding 1 tablespoon butter halfway, and turning once, about 8 minutes, set aside.

In skillet, over medium heat, add remaining tablespoon olive oil. Cook remaining minced onion till softened, about 5 minutes. Add remaining 1 tablespoon butter, 1 tablespoon Worcestershire, then whisk in flour till just combined. Slowly whisk in beef broth over medium heat till gravy thickens as preferred, at least 5 minutes.

For each serving, place ½ cup cooked rice in a bowl, stir in some of the scallions. Top with patty, drizzle all with gravy. Top with fried egg and more scallions.

Tuna Bora Bora with South Seas Coconut Sauce

Makes 4 servings

TUNA

4 high-quality fresh tuna steaks, about 3 pounds total weight

Marinade for Tuna
¼ cup sesame oil (canola will do in a pinch)
Juice of 2 limes (or 3 if they're small)
1 tablespoon red chili paste
2 cloves garlic minced fine
2 tablespoons soy sauce
In small bowl, whisk marinade ingredients together and let sit for 30 to 60 minutes before using.

¼ cup white and ¼ cup black sesame seeds (combined in a large flat soup bowl or on a big plate)
¼ cup sesame oil for searing (canola will do in a pinch)

Heat oven to 275°F.

Salt and pepper both sides of steaks, press seasoning into flesh so it stays during marinade. To keep your salt and pepper dispensers away from fishy hands, add about ½ teaspoon salt and ½ teaspoon pepper for each steak in a small bowl in advance, and use your fingers to sprinkle on steaks as needed. Do not oversalt.

In large skillet (non-stick is best) heat 2 tablespoons oil on medium-high till shimmering. Dip one steak in marinade, coating all sides, then dredge in sesame seeds to cover. Steak does not have to be entirely and perfectly covered, you will lose some of the seeds in the pan during cooking anyway.

Sear first steak in pan, about 2 minutes per side unless your steaks are thin in which case 1 minute each side. Using 2 forks to turn, sear all flat sides of the steak so no pink remains. Cook second steak. Add remaining 2 tablespoons oil, heat till shimmering, cook remaining two steaks. Transfer four steaks to heat-safe pan, keep warm in oven while you make the sauce.

SAUCE

1 tablespoon sesame oil (canola will do in a pinch)
1 tablespoon red chili paste
1 clove garlic, minced fine
1 teaspoon grated fresh ginger (or ground from a jar if you must)
1 can (14 ounces) coconut milk
Juice of 2 limes (or 3 if they're small)
2 tablespoons soy sauce
1 teaspoon cornstarch

In medium skillet, or pan you may have just cooked the fish in, heat oil. When oil is heated add the chili paste and let it cook for a minute. It may spatter a bit so give it room! Then add the garlic and ginger and cook for a few minutes. Do not burn. Add the milk, lime juice, soy sauce, and cornstarch. Simmer on medium-high heat about 7 or 8 minutes till milk mixture reduces a bit and the cornstarch thickens it up.

To serve: make a pool of the coconut sauce on the plate and rest tuna steak in it. You can also flip a molded scoop of sticky rice onto the plate, then pool the sauce, then add the tuna with some sugar snap peas beside it. Garnish with sliced scallions on the fish, and lime wedges on the side, if desired.

Pork Chops Bali Ha'i

Makes 4 servings

Here am I, your special pork chops, come to me, come to me.
— *Adapted from Oscar Hammerstein II*

4 bone-in pork chops, 1-inch thick, about 2 pounds total

1 can (20 ounces) pineapple chunks, drained, reserving
 2 tablespoons juice

Coarse salt and freshly ground pepper

1 tablespoon peanut or canola oil

2 cloves garlic, minced

1 small onion, halved and cut in crescents

2 tablespoons port wine

¾ cup apple sauce

2 tablespoons chili sauce

1 tablespoon soy sauce

1 tablespoon brown sugar

1 tablespoon apple cider vinegar

1 tablespoon arrowroot starch or cornstarch mixed with
 2 tablespoons pineapple juice

4 scallions, green part only, sliced, divided

Heat oven to 350°F. Pre-measure all ingredients into individual small bowls or other measures.

Salt and pepper both sides of chops. In an oven-friendly large skillet over medium-high heat, heat 1 tablespoon oil, add chops, cook till nicely colored on all six sides, about 15 minutes. Place skillet with chops in oven. Bake till chops no longer pink in center, about 8 minutes.

Transfer chops to a plate. Remember pan handle is *very hot!* To pan, over medium heat, add garlic and onion, stir to coat with drippings. Cook till softened, about 4 minutes. Meanwhile, re-stir pineapple juice arrowroot mixture. Then, stirring after each addition, add port, apple sauce, chili sauce, soy sauce, sugar, vinegar, the starch and pineapple juice mixture. Stir till thickened, about 30 seconds.

Return chops to pan, add one half the scallions and all the pineapple chunks. Cook for 4 minutes, turning chops once. Run pan under broiler till pineapple has a bit of color but is not burnt, 2 to 3 minutes. Garnish with remaining scallions and serve.

NATIONAL
HAWAII DAY:
JULY 5

Hawaiian Macaroni Salad

Makes 6 to 8 servings

2 cups elbow macaroni, cooked following package instructions

¼ cup apple cider vinegar

⅔ cup mayonnaise

¼ cup whole milk

1 tablespoon brown sugar

1 teaspoon soy sauce

3 scallions, white and green parts, sliced on the diagonal

2 medium carrots, grated (using box grater)

½ teaspoon salt

½ teaspoon freshly ground pepper

To large mixing bowl add hot macaroni, pour vinegar over, stir. Add mayo, milk, sugar, soy sauce, combine thoroughly. Reserving a few teaspoons of onions and carrots for garnish, add the rest to mac mixture, stir. Mix in salt and pepper. Cover and refrigerate at least an hour, or overnight, before enjoying.

Baked Beans Aloha

Makes 6 to 8 servings

2 tablespoons butter, divided

1 can (6 ounces) tomato paste

¼ cup brown sugar

2 tablespoons molasses

2 tablespoons classic yellow mustard

½ teaspoon garlic powder

1 tablespoon apple cider vinegar

1 medium onion, chopped fine

½ pound ham steak, cut in ½-inch cubes

1 can (20 ounces) pineapple tidbits, well drained

2 cans (16 ounces each) great northern beans

Couple dashes favorite hot sauce, to taste

Grease a 2-quart baking dish with a tablespoon of butter. (Any shaped dish is fine, though I especially like round for this recipe.)

Heat oven to 350°F.

In small bowl, stir together tomato paste, sugar, molasses, mustard, garlic powder, vinegar. In medium saucepan over medium-high heat, melt the other tablespoon butter, sauté onion till softened, about 5 minutes. Add ham and cook till slightly browned, about 5 minutes. Add tomato paste mixture, pineapple, stir well.

Stir in beans, add hot sauce (optional), spoon into buttered dish, cover with foil, bake for 40 minutes.

Remove foil and bake another 10 minutes.

Pineapple Upside-Down Cake Coleman

Irresistible, moist, heavenly. Just like our Cousin Marian, you will want to eat the whole thing in one sitting. Recipe courtesy of Gray Coleman.

CAKE
7 pineapple slices
1 ½ cups unbleached, all-purpose flour
1 tablespoon baking powder
½ teaspoon salt
¼ cup (½ stick) butter, softened
¾ cup granulated sugar
1 large egg
1 teaspoon vanilla extract
½ cup milk

TOPPING
½ cup packed brown sugar, divided
7 maraschino cherries
¼ cup (½ stick) butter, melted
1 teaspoon ground cinnamon

Heat oven to 375°F. Generously coat a 9-inch round baking pan with cooking spray. Drain pineapple, reserving juice, arrange slices on paper towel-lined plate or cookie sheet and pat slices dry with towel.

Whisk together flour, baking powder, and salt, set aside. To a large bowl, add softened butter. Gradually add granulated sugar, beating with electric mixer for about 2 minutes till fluffy. Beat in egg and vanilla till fully incorporated. Beat in flour mixture in two additions. Beat in milk, blending thoroughly to finish batter. It will be thick.

Sprinkle the prepared pan with 3 tablespoons brown sugar. You may need to use your fingers if it clumps. Add pineapple slices and cherries. Mix melted butter, remaining brown sugar, and cinnamon, and pour evenly over fruit.

Carefully spoon batter over fruit. Gently smooth batter out with spoon or offset spatula most of the way to the edges of pan. Batter will soften, flooding to meet pan sides as cake bakes. Bake for 30 to 35 minutes, till golden brown and a toothpick comes out clean. Wait 5 minutes after removing from oven then invert onto plate for serving. If any of the topping comes loose just pop it right back in, nobody but you needs to know.

*Patio Party

The Line Forms Right Here Onion Dip

Makes enough for a 16-person party

This recipe uses instant and powdered spice products for convenience and flavor. And you know what? They work! Right by this dip will be the place to be at your next party, so make room . . .

8 ounces sour cream
¼ cup mayonnaise
1 heaping tablespoon instant diced onion
½ teaspoon onion powder
¼ teaspoon garlic powder
¼ teaspoon salt
1 tablespoon dried parsley (or fresh)
2 large or 3 smaller scallions, thinly sliced white and green parts, save some of the green for garnish
Couple dashes hot sauce

Mix it all up, chill for a few hours or overnight, then serve garnished with sliced green scallions. Present with ruffle chips—the kind that have ridges!

Double Grapefruit Sputnik Snack Ship

Makes enough for a 25-person party

The height of mid-century snack swank.

> 2 large well-shaped, blemish-free grapefruits
> 2 sticks (6 ounces each) pepperoni, sliced bite-size
> 8 ounce block sharp cheddar or pepper jack cheese,
>   cut in bite-sized pieces
> Small pimento stuffed olives (optional)
> Loose leaf lettuce and grape tomatoes for presentation
> Toothpicks (extra credit for multicolored)

On your glorious serving plate or tray of choice, arrange lettuce, place grapefruits side by side. With toothpicks, skewer pepperoni, cheese, and olive, if using. Leave enough toothpick on end of each "skewer" for guest to pull with. Poke each into grapefruits in attractive pattern. With each bite you get the savory of the meat and cheese, plus the sweet of the fruit!

Oeufs Diablo (*Deviled Eggs*)

Makes 24 servings

Hard boiling eggs can bring on episodes of high anxiety if you don't know what you're doing. Just ask my close friends. Follow this recipe and you should emerge triumphant.

- 1 tablespoon salt
- 2 tablespoons distilled white vinegar
- 12 large eggs
- ¼ cup mayonnaise
- 2 teaspoons Dijon mustard
- 2 tablespoons butter, softened
- 1 teaspoon white vinegar
- 1 teaspoon sugar
- 1 teaspoon finely ground pepper
- 1 ½ tablespoons finely minced parsley
- Smoked paprika for garnish
- 1 ½ tablespoons minced chives for garnish

In large pot, bring three inches water, salt, and vinegar to a rolling boil. With slotted, or other spoon place eggs in water, reduce heat to a simmer, cook 12 to 13 minutes uncovered. Plunge eggs in large bowl of ice water for 5 minutes. Tap each on flat end to break shell then peel under the cold water in the bowl.

Slice in half lengthwise. Remove yolks to a medium bowl. Add mayo, mustard, butter, vinegar, sugar, pepper, parsley, mash together thoroughly with a fork and/or spoon till smooth enough to pipe (no chunks or lumps). Be patient, and vigorous.

Into a pastry bag with large open star tip (not too narrow on end), spoon mixture then pipe into each of the whites. Top each with a sprinkle of paprika and a pinch of chives and serve to a 21-gun salute.

CELERY BOATS

You'll need: a bunch of celery, slice ribs into 2 to 3-inch pieces. 2 (8 ounces each) packages cream cheese, softened. Season with 2 teaspoons onion powder and 1 teaspoon pepper, pipe into celery slices. Garnish with sprinkle of paprika or diced pimentos. Serves 15 to 20.

Toe-Curlin' Creole Cocktail Sauce

Enough for a great big platter's worth of shrimp dippin'.

- **10 ounces organic, or "simply" ketchup**
- **3 tablespoons prepared horseradish, HOT preferred**
- **Juice of one lemon**
- **1 tablespoon Worcestershire sauce**
- **2 tablespoons dehydrated Creole or Cajun Trinity with Garlic**
- **1 tablespoon cracked black pepper**

Put it all in a bowl and stir vigorously. Chill for a few hours covered, or best overnight. Watch your jubilant guests' hair stand on end at your next Shrimp Cocktail party.

When it's time for Cocktails

An occasion for cocktails should have a higher purpose. Drinks are designed to loosen things up but they shouldn't be the beginning and end reason for a party. Think of why you're partying. Is it: I want all my friends who don't know each other yet, to meet? Or are you celebrating an important life milestone or a birthday or a holiday?

Consider how many people you will have and plan accordingly. Plan for each person to have 2 drinks per hour. Multiply number of guests by number of hours your party will last by 2 drinks each and you will have *more* than enough resources on hand (30 people x 3 hours x 2 drinks = 180). Sounds like a lot of drinks! Think about your liquor choices and do the per-drink math accordingly. If you have a theme drink (always a great idea) assume it will be popular and "pour" your resources into that. You can also mix up a ton of a theme drink in advance and refrigerate. If it's more of an open bar, use what you know about your crowd's alcohol preferences to plan. Have at least whiskey, gin, vodka, tequila on hand with club soda, tonic, and orange juice for mixers. Have soft drinks for non-drinkers. Prosecco is a very popular sparkling wine these days and lends itself well to mixing, such as in the always popular Aperol Spritz. Pro Tip: you can never have too much ice.

Serve food! This is an essential part of a great cocktail get-together. If you have a theme, use it! A Cinco de Mayo party would have Mexican finger foods, a Taste of Japan party, sushi. Find out what the honoree (if there is one) likes best for snacks and prepare those. The list of delectable nibbles for the average summer or patio party is endless. Consult this chapter for a few great ideas!

Make sure you have a plan for who will bartend (sometimes setting it all out for the guests to do it even works) and who will tend the food table and bus empties. If you're not hiring people to do that, deputize a guest, or four, to take turns watching over a few party tasks.

And, as I always say: *decorate*. It doesn't have to be complicated or fancy, just enough to set a festive tone.

Always drink responsibly. Call a car for guests that might have enjoyed your swank affair a bit too much.

Theme cocktail napkins and vintage
snack sets make a party festive!

Chicken Salad Lettuce Cups

Makes 4 to 6 "cups"

- 2 to 3 large boneless skinless chicken breasts (about 2 pounds)
- 1 dry pint grape tomatoes, cut in half
- 1 small red onion, chopped fine
- 1 large or 2 medium ribs celery, chopped fine
- ⅔ cup flat leaf parsley, chopped fine
- ½ cup mayonnaise
- Juice of one lemon
- 2 tablespoons red wine vinegar
- 1 tablespoon sugar
- ½ teaspoon garlic powder
- Bibb or Boston lettuce
- 1 teaspoon smoked paprika, for garnish
- Salt

In medium saucepan, cover chicken breasts in well-salted cold water by one inch. Bring to boil then simmer 10 minutes. Check that chicken is no longer pink in center, stop the cooking by plunging in an ice bath, cut in bite-size pieces.

To a large bowl, add chicken, tomatoes, onion, celery, parsley. Add mayo, lemon, vinegar, sugar, garlic powder. Stir all together thoroughly. Chill chicken salad at least one hour.

Divide by four or more and serve in "cups" of Bibb or Boston lettuce. Garnish with sprinkling of paprika.

Hit The Spot Gazpacho

Makes 6 servings

- 1 large cucumber, peeled, seeded, and chopped
- 2 cloves garlic, chopped
- 2 cans (14.5 ounces each) whole peeled tomatoes with juice
- 1 large green bell pepper, seeded, chopped
- 1 tablespoon sliced pickled jalapeño pepper
- ¼ cup fresh cilantro, chopped
- ½ teaspoon ground cumin
- Juice of 1 lime
- ¼ cup red wine vinegar
- 3 scallions, white and green parts, sliced thin

In food processor, place cucumber, garlic, tomatoes, bell pepper, jalapeño, cilantro. Pulse till finely chopped to your preferred consistency, but not puréed.

To large bowl, add vegetable mixture. Add cumin, lime, vinegar, scallions, stir thoroughly.

Refrigerate, covered, for at least 6 hours before serving.

Cool Crab and Avocado Knolls

Makes 4 to 6 servings

A Crabmeat Ravigote on top of an avocado salad in the shape of a round hillock, or knoll.

- 2 ripe avocados, cut into ½-inch chunks
- 3 tablespoons mayonnaise, divided
- Juice of 1 large lemon, divided
- 1 teaspoon salt, divided
- 1 pound lump crabmeat (not jumbo)
- 1 teaspoon Creole or spicy brown mustard
- Couple dashes hot sauce
- ½ cup thinly sliced scallions, white and green parts, for garnish
- 1 can (16 ounces) of baked beans; or any can with both a top and bottom on which a normal can opener will work
- Smoked paprika for garnish

To a medium bowl, add avocados, 1 tablespoon mayonnaise, juice of ½ lemon, ½ teaspoon salt. Stir and refrigerate.

To a second bowl, add crabmeat, 2 tablespoons mayonnaise, mustard, ½ teaspoon salt, hot sauce, juice of ½ lemon, refrigerate.

With can opener remove top and bottom of the can of beans. In a storage container refrigerate beans, eat when you next get the munchies. The aluminum bean can now becomes your mold.

Place mold on attractive serving plate and spray inside of mold lightly with cooking spray. If making 4 servings, press ¼ of avocado mixture into mold, or a sixth of mixture if 6 servings, etc. Next, press in ¼ to a sixth of crab mixture, as appropriate. Sprinkle top with smoked paprika, remove mold. Top with scallions. Make as many more knolls as required, serve.

Gala Concept Parties

Treasure Hunt - write clues that will lead teams of guests around your neighborhood in pursuit of the treasure. When they find each location described by a clue, an appointed person at that location gives them the next clue. Whomever gets to the final destination first, wins the big prize.

Movie or TV Show-themed - I happen to have had an unforgettable *Jungle Book* party when I was seven.

Desert Island - guests dress in grunged out clothes. What's the one dish you'd take along? The one song? The one book?

Planting Party - have everyone over to help you plant your annuals.

Picnic - pack your basket with gingham and goodies and head out to the park.

Foreign City - plan ahead if you're traveling with friends: Marrakech, London, Tokyo . . . Take theme decorations and appropriate country flag food picks, have special cocktail napkins printed!

Holiday Brunch at a Restaurant - e.g. take candle holders with pastel candles, plastic eggs, small arrangements of spring tulips for an Easter lunch.

Hobby Party - stamp collecting, scrapbooking, let's all do it together!

Doggy Party - have all your friends bring their dogs (or birds! or bunnies!) over. If you have a big backyard, and/or if your house can take it! Have fun planning food for the pets!

Captain Nemo's Hot Curry Crab Dip
Makes 24 servings

The favorite snack of Indian prince Captain Nemo, whenever he goes on those long trips 20,000 leagues under the sea. Nemo may be Latin for "no one," but that won't describe the crowd of guests surrounding this tasty seafood treat at your next summer get-together!

- 1 pound lump crabmeat, cleaned and picked
- ⅔ cup marinated artichokes, chopped
- 1 red bell pepper, diced
- 8 ounces pepper jack cheese, grated (with hand grater)
- 1 cup shredded or grated Parmesan cheese
- ⅔ cup mayonnaise
- ¾ cup scallions, sliced thin, white and green parts
- 2 heaping tablespoons curry powder
- 1 teaspoon salt
- 1 tablespoon freshly ground pepper
- Juice of one lemon
- Paprika, for garnish

Heat oven to 350°F. In large bowl, thoroughly fold together all ingredients except paprika. Spray a 4-cup capacity casserole or other baking dish with cooking spray. Spoon mixture into dish, sprinkle lightly but evenly with paprika and bake on middle rack, uncovered, for 30 minutes. Let rest out of oven for 20 minutes. Serve with celery or carrot sticks, a sliced baguette, or any other crackers or chips you prefer.

Cold English Pea Salad

Makes 6 to 8 side servings

- 3 slices bacon, cooked till just crisp, then crumbled
- 1 package (20 ounces) frozen sweet peas, thawed
- 1 cup cheddar cheese, cut in pea-sized cubes
- 1 large or 2 medium ribs celery, chopped fine
- ½ small red onion, chopped fine
- 2 large hard-boiled eggs, chopped
- ⅓ cup mayonnaise
- 1 teaspoon sugar
- 1 tablespoon apple cider vinegar
- Salt and freshly ground pepper to taste

Mix it all up, refrigerate one hour.

Brian's Lip-Smacking Catalina Dressing

Fresh celery and lemon juice make this one sing.

- ¼ cup organic or "simply" ketchup
- ¼ cup sugar
- ¼ cup red wine vinegar
- ¼ cup chopped shallot
- ¼ cup chopped celery (1 large or 2 medium ribs)
- 1 tablespoon fresh lemon juice
- 1 teaspoon Worcestershire sauce
- 1 heaping teaspoon paprika (not smoked)
- ½ teaspoon each salt and freshly ground pepper
- ½ cup canola oil

In blender, cover and combine all ingredients except oil. Process till smooth. Add oil, re-cover. At lowest speed, pulse till fully blended. Refrigerate at least 3 hours so vegetable ingredients absorb other flavors. Keep in fridge up to 3 days.

INDEPENDENCE DAY:
JULY 4

Delmonico Ribeye with Herb Butter

Makes 2 to 4 servings (It's a lot of food.)

The classic.

Two 20-ounce ribeye steaks

½ cup (1 stick) fresh unsalted butter, softened

¼ cup chopped chives

½ small shallot, minced

A few squeezes of fresh lemon juice

Canola olive oil blend

Kosher salt and freshly ground pepper

Let the meat sit out for 30 to 45 minutes before you season. Heat oven to 450°F.

While steaks sit, in a small bowl, combine butter, chives, shallots, lemon juice, salt and pepper to taste. Roll into small log, cover in plastic, put in freezer to firm up (but not freeze solid), about 30 minutes. Salt and pepper steaks generously all over, set aside.

In cast iron or other heavy oven-proof skillet, add a few tablespoons oil over medium-high heat. Using tongs, sear all over, including sides, about 7 minutes total.

Place pan with steaks in upper half of oven, about 5 minutes each side (flip once) for medium rare, 8 minutes each side (flip once) for medium. Ovens may vary.

Rest out of oven for 10 minutes.

Cut butter in half if serving 2 persons, or more, depending. Top steaks with butter.

In a low oven, briefly melt butter on top of steaks, serve.

Billy Oliva is one of America's top chefs, helming the country's first fine-dining restaurant, Delmonico's. The legendary institution, older than the Statue of Liberty, is the birthplace of Lobster Newburg, Baked Alaska, Eggs Benedict, and, of course, the Delmonico Ribeye.

Chef Billy and his culinary expertise are regularly featured on national food and entertainment programs. He focuses on keeping menus current with seasonal, farm-to-table ingredients. The Delmonico brothers were actually pioneers of the farm-to-table concept when they first opened in the 19th century.

Once the steak hits the pan we leave it alone.

My first question is about steak because we know you're the King of Steak. What are the essential things to know if you're cooking a steak using your stovetop and oven at home?

Buy the best beef. It's graded select, choice, and prime, prime being best. Go to a good butcher. Get choice or prime. The rib eye, which is the classic Delmonico cut, has a high fat content, is highly marbled, which is best in terms of flavor and taste. And when we say fat and marbling, we're talking about striations of white that run through the meat. In terms of cooking that in a pan, beef takes very well to a good cast iron skillet. And beef needs to be at room temperature. Very important, you never take it out of the refrigerator and slap it right into the pan. No. It will tighten up and lose a lot of juice. Room temperature beef's going to relax. Next is seasoning. Home cooks need to season properly. Salt is key, a good quality salt. I'm not talking about iodized table salt. You want a kosher or a sea salt, which a lot of people at home don't have. Then for cooking steaks in a cast iron pan, we always start with a little bit of oil. I like to use about two tablespoons of a blended canola-olive. And once the steak hits the pan, we leave it alone. Once you have a nice caramelized brown color, then you flip it once. You want to get that same sear on the other side. Now, depending on cooking temperature, a rare or a medium-rare steak's not going to go in an oven to finish. It'll be finished on top in the pan. Once you flip it, you can always make it taste better, right? We're going to take two tablespoons of a high-fat European butter, a clove of garlic, some fresh thyme, and all that's going to go into that pan with the seared steak to baste.

Would you pepper when you're doing your salt?

Yes. We use a whole black pepper here to start, and white pepper, and kosher salt. We finish with Morton's sea salt and La Boïte Pierre Poivre. The Poivre peppercorns are almost floral, not spicy. Then remember, when you take it out of the pan, the steak's still cooking. You need to rest it, ten minutes. Resting is the number one thing people don't do.

What would be one of your favorite summer cookout-type side dishes?

I grew up with a very Italian background. My father was Sicilian. So one of the things that was always around was cold pasta. Tortellini was a favorite. With pesto or olive oil, artichokes. In the summertime, it'd be tomatoes, basil.

If you had to improve some sort of traditional, warm weather recipe for cocktail hour, like deviled eggs or cocktail weenies, what would you do?

One of the most requested things in this restaurant is cocktail franks. So, a cool way to dress them up, we will take a caramelized onion mix, sauerkraut, and mustard and do a stuffed pigs in a blanket.

That sounds outstanding! Delmonico's is famous for originating popular dishes. What recipe of your own have you added that you think might become one of those enduring favorites?

The house-cured bacon that we do. It's cured in a maple bourbon. It's then smoked for about 9, 10 hours. And then it's sous vide, and then it's glazed. It's fork tender. You don't need a knife to cut it. We ran that as a special here, and the response was ridiculous. We could probably never take that off the menu. It's just turned into a thing that people expect.

Who was the best cook in your family, and why?

I'm going to say my mom.

What made her stand out? Was it her work ethic, her curiosity, her technique?

Her work ethic. We used to have sometimes 30 or 40 people over. She was good at organizing and getting stuff done.

Is there anything else you'd tell the home cook to make their dishes better?

When you're baking, you need to follow the recipe. Cooking fish or chicken or steak, you have your ingredients. If you like more garlic, you can add more garlic. You know, there's nothing set in stone. I tell people here all the time, and I've even said it to you, I make it up as I go along sometimes. And that doesn't hurt.

Fiesta Mexicana

Salsa Pancho Villa

Makes 4 cups salsa

Let's get this fiesta started! Like its namesake, you can start your own revolution with this Mexican ambrosia. It will rock your world.

1 can (28 ounces) whole peeled tomatoes

1 large onion, roughly chopped

3 bell peppers, 1 each green, yellow, orange, roughly chopped

4 ounces pickled jalapeño peppers

4 ounces canned green chiles

Big handful fresh cilantro

Juice of 2 limes

2 tablespoons apple cider vinegar

1 teaspoon ground cumin

In food processor, in batches, pulse tomatoes, onion, cilantro, bell peppers, jalapeño, chiles. Add all to large bowl. Add lime juice, vinegar, cumin, stir vigorously. Let chill for several hours before serving so flavors blend.

Taquería Taco Meat Seasoning

Replaces those store-bought packets. Makes 3 tablespoons, enough for three taco nights!

1 tablespoon chili powder

1 tablespoon sugar

2 teaspoons ground cumin

1 tablespoon minced dried onions, or 1 teaspoon onion powder

1 teaspoon dried oregano

1 teaspoon smoked paprika

1 teaspoon coarse ground black pepper

½ teaspoon garlic powder

¼ teaspoon cayenne pepper

Combine all ingredients. For every ½ to 1 pound of meat, add 1 to 1 ½ tablespoons of the seasoning, with ¼ cup water, to frying pan. Cook meat till done. Great for beef, pork, chicken, even Mexican grasshoppers.

Decorate!

If you're having a theme dinner, decorate! There are plenty of ways to do it. Go to your nearest party or craft store and find a few inexpensive items that are appropriate to your international or holiday theme. Pick up some lanterns for China, flower garlands for spring, Easter, or a luau, and fall flowers and gourds for Halloween and Thanksgiving.

Search your favorite online retail site for a jackpot of apropos swag. Use a country's national flag as a tablecloth to set the theme (see Mexico, above). Go to consumer-to-consumer sites that deal in old items and collectibles to score jaw-dropping vintage pieces of serving ware that make every occasion special.

You can never have too much of these: festive food picks and skewers, vintage barware and swizzle sticks, gala centerpieces and flower arrangements, awesome mood lighting, ethnic props and buntings.

Seven Layer Dip for a Crowd

Makes 6 to 8 servings

File this one under Tex-Mex. I take this to parties in a big pan, about 17 x 13 x 3 inches. I buy pre-made salsa and guacamole but you could multiply the recipes in this chapter. Go with 1 ½ times the salsa recipe and double the guacamole.

- 3 cans (4 ounces each) diced green chiles
- 4 cans (15.4 ounces each) organic refried beans
- 2 bunches green onions, white and green parts, sliced
- 1 jar (10 ounces) colossal pimiento-stuffed olives, sliced
- 2 containers (16 ounces each) sour cream
- 1 package taco seasoning (2 tablespoons)—or make it yourself—see recipe prior page
- 3 cans (15.5 ounces each) black beans, drained
- 3 jars (15 to 16 ounces each) medium salsa
- 32 ounces guacamole
- 16 ounces shredded Mexican blend cheese
- 3 bags (13 ounces each) tortilla chips. Extra credit for lime flavor!

In a medium pot, over medium-high heat, stir chiles in with refried beans and cook till hot, about 5 minutes, set aside to cool. Mix 2 tablespoons taco seasoning in with the sour cream. 7-layer order, from bottom up: refried beans, guacamole, black beans, salsa, sour cream, cheese, onions, and olives. Refrigerate till serving.

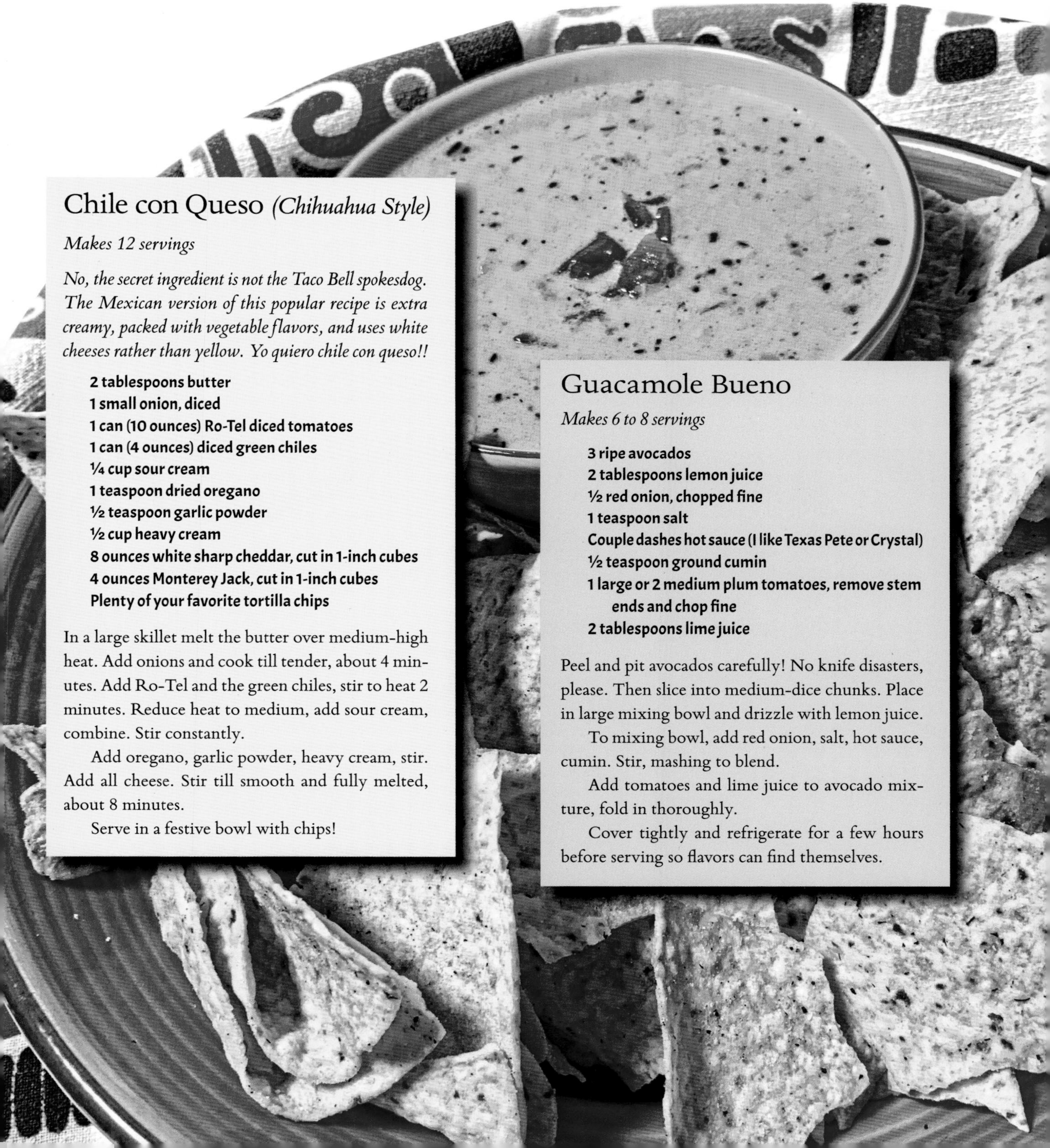

Chile con Queso *(Chihuahua Style)*

Makes 12 servings

No, the secret ingredient is not the Taco Bell spokesdog. The Mexican version of this popular recipe is extra creamy, packed with vegetable flavors, and uses white cheeses rather than yellow. Yo quiero chile con queso!!

**2 tablespoons butter
1 small onion, diced
1 can (10 ounces) Ro-Tel diced tomatoes
1 can (4 ounces) diced green chiles
¼ cup sour cream
1 teaspoon dried oregano
½ teaspoon garlic powder
½ cup heavy cream
8 ounces white sharp cheddar, cut in 1-inch cubes
4 ounces Monterey Jack, cut in 1-inch cubes
Plenty of your favorite tortilla chips**

In a large skillet melt the butter over medium-high heat. Add onions and cook till tender, about 4 minutes. Add Ro-Tel and the green chiles, stir to heat 2 minutes. Reduce heat to medium, add sour cream, combine. Stir constantly.

Add oregano, garlic powder, heavy cream, stir. Add all cheese. Stir till smooth and fully melted, about 8 minutes.

Serve in a festive bowl with chips!

Guacamole Bueno

Makes 6 to 8 servings

**3 ripe avocados
2 tablespoons lemon juice
½ red onion, chopped fine
1 teaspoon salt
Couple dashes hot sauce (I like Texas Pete or Crystal)
½ teaspoon ground cumin
1 large or 2 medium plum tomatoes, remove stem ends and chop fine
2 tablespoons lime juice**

Peel and pit avocados carefully! No knife disasters, please. Then slice into medium-dice chunks. Place in large mixing bowl and drizzle with lemon juice.

To mixing bowl, add red onion, salt, hot sauce, cumin. Stir, mashing to blend.

Add tomatoes and lime juice to avocado mixture, fold in thoroughly.

Cover tightly and refrigerate for a few hours before serving so flavors can find themselves.

Piggy Chalupas

Makes 6 to 8 servings

I call these "piggy" chalupas because they've pork in them but also because they so delicious you will eat them like you are a pig. Chalupa means "canoe" in Spanish. Chalupas sail, er, hail originally from Puebla, Mexico.

½ pound ground pork
1 tablespoon Taquería Taco Meat Seasoning (recipe this chapter)
1 can (16 ounces) refried beans, heated
1 head iceberg lettuce sliced thin

6 scallions sliced thin, white and a bit of green parts
1 cup chopped cilantro
5 ounces queso fresco, chopped bite-size
4-inch yellow corn tortillas, about 24
Canola oil
Salsa verde
Salsa roja
Pickled jalapeño slices (optional)

To a large skillet over medium-high heat, add ground pork, taco seasoning, and ¼ cup water. Cook till meat is done, about 7 minutes. Set to one side in a serving bowl. Heat refried beans in a small pot, keep on hand.

To skillet, add canola oil till bottom of skillet is just covered. Heat over medium-high till shimmering.

Working quickly, fry three tortillas at a time. Beware of hot oil spattering. As tortillas cook in the oil, to the top of each tortilla add green or red salsa, then some beans, then some pork if you choose. After about two minutes, using a long-handled spatula, remove each tortilla full of ingredients to a paper towel-lined plate or baking sheet. The tortillas will have become crispy like a tostada and the edges should have curled slightly, like a raft or boat. You may need to add just a bit more oil for further batches. Guests should then pile them up with the rest of the toppings. These chalupas are so yummy they'll surely be rowing back for more!

LA CHALUPA

Tacos de Pescado (Fish Tacos)

Pan-seared fish with a delicious slaw. One of my FAVORITE recipes.

Makes 8 servings

- 1 cup sour cream
- 2 teaspoons chili powder
- ½ teaspoon garlic powder
- 1 large cucumber, peeled, seeded, thinly sliced (about 1 ½ cups)
- 1 red onion, thinly sliced (about 2 cups)
- 2 tablespoons pickled jalapeño slices, minced
- ½ small green cabbage, cored and sliced thin (about 4 cups)
- 1 large beefsteak-style tomato, seeded and chopped

- ¼ cup orange juice
- 3 tablespoons lime juice
- ¼ cup apple cider vinegar
- ½ teaspoon salt
- 1 ½ pounds mahi mahi or cod, cut in 1 ½-inch square pieces (about 24 pieces)
- 2 tablespoons Old Bay seasoning
- Twelve 6-inch corn tortillas
- 2 to 3 tablespoons canola oil
- 1 almost ripe avocado, diced

Crema: Stir together sour cream and 2 teaspooons chili powder, garlic powder, chill. *Slaw*: Combine cucumber, onion, jalapeño, cabbage, tomato, chill. *Dressing*: Whisk together orange juice, lime juice, vinegar, salt, chill.

Heat oven to 300°F. Divide 12 tortillas into 2 foil-covered packages and heat for 10 minutes when oven is ready.

Season fish with Old Bay, tossing to coat. In large cast iron skillet or other heavy pan, heat 2 tablespoons oil. Cook each piece, all sides, about 4 minutes total, don't crowd pan. Set aside and keep warm.

Fill a tortilla with fish and avocado, top with sour cream, add the salad and drizzle top with dressing. You won't be able to eat just one!

NATIONAL TACO DAY: OCTOBER 4

Gran Gusto Enchilada Sauce

Makes 4 cups

- ½ teaspoon salt
- 1 tablespoon dried oregano
- 1 teaspoon ground cumin
- ½ teaspoon garlic powder
- 3 tablespoons olive oil
- 2 tablespoons all-purpose flour
- 2 tablespoons chili powder (make sure is not super hot)
- 3 cups vegetable broth
- 1 can (8 ounces) tomato sauce
- 1 can (6 ounces) tomato paste
- 1 tablespoon apple cider vinegar

In small bowl stir together salt, oregano, cumin, garlic powder. In a large saucepan heat olive oil over medium-high heat till shimmering. Add flour and chili powder. Whisk constantly till mixture looks oily, about 1 minute. Lowering heat slightly, thoroughly incorporate salt and spice mixture, another 30 seconds.

Pan is hot: to avoid spattering, carefully whisk in half the broth. Add tomato sauce and paste, whisk frequently, cooking 3 minutes. Add remaining half broth. Stir in vinegar, simmer over medium heat till sauce thickens, 8 to 10 minutes. Let cool. Best to let the flavors meld for a few hours covered in fridge, then time to make enchiladas!

Stacked Beef Enchiladas

Makes 4 servings

Inspired by my sister Kate's renowned recipe.

- 2 tablespoons canola oil
- 1 small onion diced
- 1 clove garlic, minced
- 1 pound ground beef, 80% lean
- 2 tablespoons chili powder
- ½ teaspoon cumin
- ⅓ cup all-purpose flour
- 1 cup beef broth
- At least 2 cups Gran Gusto Enchilada Sauce (recipe at left)
- At least twelve 6-inch corn tortillas
- 1 ½ cups shredded cheddar cheese (shred this from a block at home)
- 2 cups romaine lettuce, sliced thin
- ½ cup sliced scallions, white and green parts
- ⅓ cup sliced black olives

In large cast iron or other skillet, over medium-high heat, heat 2 tablespoons oil. Add onion, garlic, cook 4 minutes till softened. Add beef and cook just till no longer pink. Stir in chili powder and cumin. Stir in flour. Add broth. Simmer, stirring frequently as mixture thickens, 5 minutes. Set aside and keep warm.

Heat oven to 350°F. For each stack: in medium skillet over medium heat, heat ½ cup Gran Gusto sauce for each three tortillas. When sauce starts to steam, dip each tortilla in sauce with tongs, about 5 seconds per side. Keep warm on a sheet pan nearby. Repeat.

To build your stack: place one tortilla on sheet pan, top with beef and cheese, top with second tortilla, add more beef and cheese, add third tortilla, top with cheese. Place in oven for 3 minutes uncovered, to heat stack and melt cheese. Remove with wide spatula to serving plate and top with shredded lettuce, scallions and olive. Hashtag: que delicioso!

Harvest Moon

Texas Hayride

Baytown Biscuits

Makes 24 biscuits

When I was just a little Texan, my Grandma Hittie was culinary director for the Episcopal retreat at Camp Allen, on Trinity Bay near Baytown. A treasured memory. These biscuits are named for there. I recommend you get yourself some apple butter. It was a favorite on toast when I was growing up. With these biscuits, a real treat!

> **5 cups unbleached all-purpose flour**
> **2 ½ tablespoons baking powder**
> **1 teaspoon baking soda**
> **2 tablespoons sugar**
> **1 teaspoon salt**
> **1 cup lard or vegetable shortening**
> **4 tablespoons (½ stick) chilled butter, cut in ¼-inch pieces**
> **2 cups buttermilk**
> **1 large egg**

Heat oven to 425°F. Lightly grease or spray two baking sheets.

In medium bowl whisk together flour, baking powder, soda, sugar, salt. Add lard or shortening. With a crossing motion, use two knives to cut fat into small bits. Using your fingers combine lard thoroughly with the flour. Do not overdo this. Add the squares of chilled butter, work in with fingers till just incorporated. Don't worry if you still have clumps of butter, this will increase flakiness. Put the bowl in the freezer for ten minutes to firm up the butter again.

Make a well in the center of dry ingredients, add buttermilk. Flour your hands and knead dough gently several times in bowl. Dough will stick to your hands. Hang in there. Don't overhandle. Transfer dough to lightly floured surface. Flour your hands and pat dough out into a ¾-inch thick rectangle. Fold one third of the rectangle in over the center, then fold the other third in over that. This creates layers in the final biscuits. Now pat out again to ¾-inch thick. Using a 2 ½-inch cutter start cutting circles of dough, but don't twist the cutter. Place each about ½-inch apart on sheets. Bring together remaining dough and repeat no more than twice till you have about 24 biscuits. The less you handle the dough, the better the rise and texture of the biscuits. They don't have to look perfect, these are "rustic" biscuits! Whisk egg with 1 tablespoon water. Brush egg wash onto tops of biscuits.

Place baking sheets with biscuits in freezer for 7 minutes each; this will help the biscuits rise. Bake biscuits till tops are lightly golden, 14 to 16 minutes. Switch shelves and rotate pans halfway through. Ovens are different so watch closely.

Boerne Breakfast Taco Bar

Makes 4 to 6 servings

Rise and shine, it's taco time! Breakfast tacos in the Hill Country are live-without-able. Boerne is pronounced "BURN-ee" for you Texas Hill Country neophytes out there. My daddy was born in Boerne. It's worth making these potatoes from scratch. Shred the cheese yourself. Add spicy chorizo, an additional popular filling.

- 2 baking potatoes, peeled and cut into ½-inch cubes
- 8 slices thick-cut bacon
- 3 tablespoons peanut or canola oil, divided
- 1 teaspoon salt
- Freshly ground fresh pepper
- ¼ cup thinly sliced scallions, green parts only
- 2 tablespoons butter, divided
- At least eight 6-inch corn tortillas
- 1 can (16 ounces) refried beans
- 8 large eggs, well beaten
- 1 can (10 ounces) Ro-Tel tomatoes
- 1 cup (4 ounces) shredded sharp cheddar cheese
- Salsa verde

Heat oven to 250°F.

Put potatoes in medium saucepan and cover with cold water by 2 inches. Bring to boil, cover, cook till tender, about 15 minutes. Drain and pat dry on paper towels.

In large cast iron skillet fry bacon till cooked but not yet crisp, set aside. Drain and discard fat safely.

In same skillet, heat 2 tablespoons oil over medium-high heat. Add potatoes, salt, 3 grinds pepper, cook, flipping several times till potatoes start to brown, 8 minutes. Add scallions and butter, stir till potatoes are coated. Set potatoes aside, cover with foil.

Wrap tortillas in foil and heat in oven 20 minutes. In small saucepan, heat refried beans.

In clean large skillet over medium-high heat, melt 1 tablespoon butter. Add eggs, let firm up for a minute then add tomatoes. Scramble eggs softly, then promptly remove to a plate.

Present potatoes, bacon, refried beans, eggs, cheese, salsa, and tortillas in a buffet-style arrangement so folks can build their own!

Easy as Frito Pie

Makes 4 servings

It's hard to be sure whether the Frito pie was invented in Texas or New Mexico, but c'mon guys, chili is the state food of Texas! Now, sing along with me: "Ay-yi-yi-yi, I am the Frito Bandito . . ."

- 1 tablespoon canola oil
- 1 small onion, minced
- 2 cloves garlic, minced
- 1 pound ground chuck
- 1 ½ tablespoons chili powder
- 1 teaspoon ground paprika
- ½ teaspoon salt
- ¼ teaspoon ground cumin
- 1 can (8 ounces) tomato sauce
- 4 bags (1-ounce each) Frito chips
- 1 cup (4 ounces) shredded sharp cheddar cheese (shred it yourself at home)
- ½ cup sour cream
- ⅓ cup scallions, white and green parts, in ¼-inch slices

In a large skillet, over medium-high heat, heat oil, add onion and garlic, cook till softened, about 4 minutes.

Add meat, breaking it up with wooden spoon. Add chili powder, paprika, salt, cumin, stir. When meat is no longer pink, add tomato sauce. Simmer over medium heat till most liquid has evaporated, about 10 minutes. Makes 3 cups chili.

With scissors, cut open center of each Frito bag, lay each on own plate. Spoon a good helping of chili into bag on top of Fritos. Top with shredded cheese, sour cream, and a generous sprinkle of scallions. For maximum authenticity, eat with a white plastic fork. Try not to think about the fact that Anthony Bourdain once called these, and I paraphrase: a deuce in a bag. Enjoy any leftover chili for lunch tomorrow!

Good as All Git-Out Oven Brisket

Makes 4 to 6 servings. Though if you got two really hungry guys, they might could polish the whole thing off themselves. I've seen it happen. Is especially yummy with my Insalata Russa (potato salad) that goes with the Feast of Seven Fishes in the Christmas chapter.

- 3 tablespoons coarse or kosher salt
- 2 tablespoons packed brown sugar (I use dark for this)
- 1 tablespoon smoked paprika (beats that liquid smoke stuff)
- 1 teaspoon celery seed
- 1 teaspoon garlic powder
- 1 teaspoon freshly cracked black pepper
- 1 prime (4 pound) first, or flat cut brisket (not the point, or deckle cut)
- 3 cups beef broth
- 1 ½ cups Fixin' to Eat Barbecue Sauce (recipe next page)
- 1 sweet onion, sliced thick
- 4 whole peeled cloves garlic

In small bowl, combine salt, sugar, paprika, celery seed, garlic powder, pepper. Rub one half on bottom of brisket (the less fatty side), then flip, and rub remaining mixture into fatty top. Set aside at room temperature while you make the BBQ sauce (next page).

Heat oven to 275°F. In approximately 16 x 12-inch roasting pan, place 3 cups beef broth, half the BBQ sauce, then the brisket. Scatter the garlic and onion in the liquid around the meat. Cover pan in foil and place in center of oven. The foil-wrapped method is known by some as the "Texas Crutch." It will ensure a tender and juicy brisket. Don't worry, you're not cheating, you're chef'ing!

Cooking time: 4 hours for a 4 pound brisket, plus final bark phase (40 minutes). At the end of the first 4 hours, take roaster CAREFULLY out of oven: lots of hot liquid! Remove brisket with tongs/spatula to plate, then pour entire pan liquid and onion mixture into a large bowl, cool and safely discard. Kick up oven to 425°F. Carefully place brisket fat side down in roaster, on center oven rack for 7 minutes uncovered, to create a bit of "bark" on the surface. Carefully flip and repeat process with fat side up, another 7 minutes. Let rest 30 minutes out of oven tented in foil. Slice against the grain. Serve with a side of Fixin' to Eat Barbecue Sauce. Whistle a few bars of "Deep in the Heart of Texas" between bites.

Fixin' to Eat Barbecue Sauce

Makes 3 cups

Hey Grandpa, what's for supper? This totes tasty no-cook BBQ sauce, that's what! Whatever you're fixin' to eat is bound to be better with this lip-smackin' brew nearby. Put it on your greatest brisket, pork, or link for a real flavor kick!

- 1 teaspoon garlic powder
- 1 teaspoon salt
- ½ teaspoon freshly ground pepper

- 2 teaspoons celery seed
- 2 tablespoons spicy brown mustard
- Juice of one lemon
- ⅓ cup A.1. Sauce
- 3 cups tomato sauce
- 1 tablespoon brown sugar (dark is best)
- Couple dashes favorite hot sauce

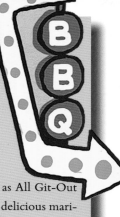

In a medium bowl, whisk energetically till all combined. Use right away as an ingredient called for in Good as All Git-Out Oven Brisket (previous page), or just store in a covered container and refrigerate for at least 3 hours to use as a delicious marinade or sauce for your next backyard shindig! It's even better the next day.

Hill Country Chicken Fried Steak and Cream Gravy

Makes 4 servings

Chili may be the official state food of Texas, but you could argue Chicken Fried Steak should win in a tie! THIS *reminds me of the "he-man" lunches my Grandma Janie made for us in the Texas Hill Country when we were growing up. Pro Tip: buy the best quality round you can find (choice or prime)—you get what you pay for.*

STEAK
- 4 top round, or cube steaks, about ½ pound each and ½-inch thick
- Coarse or kosher salt
- 2 cups all-purpose flour, divided
- 2 large eggs
- ¼ cup whole milk
- 3 tablespoons cornmeal

- 1 teaspoon seasoned salt
- 1 teaspoon chili powder
- 1 teaspoon ground paprika
- ½ teaspoon garlic powder
- 1 teaspoon freshly ground pepper
- Peanut or canola oil for frying

GRAVY
- 2 tablespoons butter
- ¼ cup all-purpose flour
- 1 ½ cups whole milk
- Salt and freshly ground pepper

Pound steaks both sides till ⅓ thinner. Blot till dry. Rub both sides steaks with ½ teaspoon coarse salt, set aside.

To deep plate or bowl add 1 cup flour. In second bowl whisk together eggs and milk. In third bowl whisk together remaining cup flour, corn meal, seasoned salt, chili powder, paprika, garlic powder.

Warm oven to 200°F. In it place sheet pan covered with paper towels to receive fried steaks.

Fill large cast iron skillet or heavy pan with oil to depth of ¼ inch. Heat oil over medium-high heat till a drop of water spatters on the surface.

Dredge each steak thoroughly in plain flour, then in egg, then in seasoned flour. Carefully place steak in hot oil. When golden brown around edges flip carefully with tongs, 3 minutes. Cook till done, 2 minutes more. Let oil come back up to temperature before next steak.

Place steaks in warm oven as you go.

Reserve 2 tablespoons of frying oil for the gravy. Safely discard rest of oil.

In clean skillet over medium heat, add reserved frying oil and butter. When just melted add flour, whisk constantly to form a light-colored roux, about 3 minutes.

Whisk in milk slowly, watching carefully for desired consistency as it starts to thicken. Salt and pepper to taste and serve immediately over steaks.

Heart of Texas Pinto Beans

Makes 8 servings. Inspired by my mother's signature dish.

- 1 pound dry pinto beans
- 1 teaspoon salt
- 1 tablespoon brown sugar
- ½ teaspoon cayenne pepper
- ½ pound thick cut smoked bacon, cut crosswise into ¼-inch strips
- 2 tablespoons salted butter
- 1 tablespoon chili powder
- 2 teaspoons onion powder
- 1 teaspoon garlic powder
- ¼ teaspoon ground cumin

In large pot, soak beans with the salt, sugar and cayenne in 6 cups water, overnight. Cover while soaking to keep out cats, bats, and other unanticipated furballs.

Next day, bring beans and their soaking water to a boil. Stir in bacon, butter, chili powder, onion powder, garlic powder, cumin.

Reduce heat to a simmer, cook, covered, for 45 minutes to 1 hour or till beans are tender, stirring occasionally.

Guadalupe Green Beans

Makes 4 to 6 servings

Named for the river that runs through the first German settlement in the Texas Hill Country, New Braunfels, this recipe celebrates the tasty Teutonic formula.

- 3 slices thick-cut bacon, cut crosswise into ¼-inch strips
- 1 small onion, diced (about ½ cup)
- ¼ cup chicken broth
- 2 tablespoons apple cider vinegar
- 1 teaspoon sugar
- ½ teaspoon freshly ground pepper
- 2 cans (14.5 ounces each) Italian cut green beans, drained

In large deep skillet, over medium-high heat, cook bacon till slightly browned but not crisp, about 5 minutes. Drain and safely discard fat. Add onion to bacon in pan, cook till softened, about 3 minutes. Add chicken broth, vinegar, sugar, pepper, then green beans. Stir over medium heat till beans absorb flavors, about 3 minutes.

Fried Okra

Makes 6 servings

As always when frying, lock up the bunnies and kittens and babies and keep 'em out of the kitchen! Hot oil is NO FUN for tinies. This recipe works beautifully with fresh okra. Frozen will pale in comparison, just say no.

- 1 cup buttermilk
- 1 cup yellow cornmeal
- ¾ cup all-purpose flour
- 1 teaspoon garlic powder
- 1 teaspoon salt
- 1 teaspoon freshly ground pepper
- 1 pound fresh okra, ends trimmed, cut in ¾-inch pieces
- Peanut or canola oil for frying

In wide shallow bowl, pour buttermilk. In second bowl, whisk together cornmeal, flour, garlic powder, salt, pepper. Prepare a paper towel-covered plate for okra when fried.

In large cast iron skillet, heat ½ inch oil to 375°F, or when bubbles form around the end of a wooden spoon held in the oil. Toss about 20 pieces okra at a time in buttermilk to coat, remove with slotted spoon, shake off excess milk, then toss to coat each piece in cornmeal mixture using a teaspoon. Use tongs to place okra in hot oil. Fry okra till golden brown, about 2 minutes per side. A fish spatula is ideal for removing okra from pan once fried. Place on paper towel-lined plate to drain. Monitor heat and adjust as needed to maintain steady frying temperature. Serve immediately.

Pedernales Pecan Pie
Makes 8 servings

Serve this wondrous dessert at Thanksgiving, or any time all year long. No corn syrup! Pro Tip: chop pecans with a sharp knife. Don't use food processor or you get dust. Nobody wants to eat your dust.

CRUST
1 ¾ cups unbleached all-purpose flour
3 tablespoons sugar
½ teaspoon salt
3 tablespoons lard, or vegetable shortening
7 tablespoons unsalted butter, cut in ¼-inch cubes, chilled
Ice water

FILLING
1 ½ cups packed brown sugar
½ cup granulated sugar
3 tablespoons unbleached all-purpose flour
3 large eggs
½ cup (1 stick) salted butter, melted
3 tablespoons milk
3 teaspoons white distilled vinegar
1 teaspoon vanilla extract
8 ounces whole pecans, reserve 40 for garnish, chop remaining by hand, about 1 ½ cups

For crust: in large bowl, whisk together flour, sugar, salt. Add lard or shortening. With a crossing motion, use two knives to cut fat into small bits. With fingers, work into flour till sandy. Work cold butter cubes into flour mixture till just combined. Add 3 tablespoons ice water, and more by the teaspoon as needed to form dough. Make sure water is fully incorporated before adding more, but don't over-knead or you will lose flakiness. Make a disk, wrap in plastic, refrigerate dough at least 30 minutes.

Heat oven to 400°F.

For 9 ½-inch pie plate, roll out dough between two sheets of parchment so it's 12 ½ inches in diameter. You may need a little flour in between the parchment for best results. Invert dough into pie plate. Fold edge of dough under to make a standing rim. To flute edge, place two fingers of one hand about ¾ inch apart inside of rim. With finger of other hand push pastry through the two fingers towards center. Repeat all the way around. Chill crust till filling is ready.

For filling: in large bowl, combine sugars and flour with your hand, breaking up any brown sugar clumps. With spoon, stir in eggs, then butter, milk, vinegar, vanilla. Stir in chopped pecans, pour mixture in crust. It will look like there's not enough, don't worry it rises quite a bit.

With the remaining whole pecans, make a sunburst or other decorative design atop the filling. The pecans float nicely.

Bake pie 10 minutes. Reduce temperature to 350°F. Bake another 30 to 35 minutes or till filling no longer jiggles when you gently shake pie. Cool completely before cutting.

Hallowe'en Goblin Fest

Great Pumpkin Soup

Makes 4 to 6 servings

The perfect treat while you wait for the superhero of pumpkin patch fame to fly in and drop off toys to all the sincere believers on Halloween night.

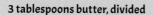

3 tablespoons butter, divided

⅓ cup raw pepitas (pumpkin seeds)

½ cup roughly chopped red onion

3 ribs celery, roughly chopped

3 medium carrots, roughly chopped

3 cloves garlic, whole

1 teaspoon ground coriander

1 teaspoon ground cumin

½ teaspoon cayenne

1 can (16 ounces) pumpkin purée (not pie mix)

2 cups vegetable broth

1 baking potato, peeled and cubed (do this at last minute so potato doesn't turn brown)

½ cup heavy cream

2 teaspoons lemon juice

In soup pot, melt 1 tablespoon butter over medium-high heat, add pepitas, a pinch of salt and sauté till one or two start to pop, about 5 minutes. Set aside.

In same pot, melt 2 tablespoons butter over medium-high heat, add onion, celery, carrots, garlic, cook 3 minutes till softened, add coriander, cumin, cayenne, and cook another two minutes. Add pumpkin, vegetable broth, potato, 1 teaspoon salt, bring to boil, then reduce heat and simmer, partially covered, for 35 minutes.

Let soup cool for 10 minutes.

Purée using immersion blender. Or use a blender or food processor but do it in batches and be careful with the hot liquid!

Reheat soup slowly, adding cream and lemon juice. Serve right away garnished with the pepitas.

Mad Scientist Beaker Blend Punch

Makes 12 servings

How does it work? The more sugar you put in each flavor of Jell-O punch, the lower the layer sinks in the pitcher, creating the psychedelic bands of a mad scientist's lab experiment!

What you'll need:

3 boxes Jell-O powder: lime, orange, grape flavors

10 tablespoons sugar

	JELL-O POWDER	SUGAR	WATER
Lime first	3 tablespoons	7 tablespoons	2 cups
Orange next	2 tablespoons	3 tablespoons	2 cups
Grape last	2 tablespoons	0 tablespoons	2 cups

Mix each punch flavor separately per the table above, chill 30 minutes. In large serving pitcher, over a lot of ice, slowly pour ⅓ lime, ⅓ orange, ⅓ grape.

Serve immediately, with your most maniacal expression. Based on your pitcher, you may have enough for seconds.

Creepy Crudités with Green Dragon Dip

Makes 2 cups dip

No dragons were harmed in the testing of this recipe.

- **2 ripe medium avocados**
- **3 tablespoons lime juice**
- **6 ounces plain fat-free Greek yogurt (¾ cup)**
- **½ teaspoon prepared wasabi**
- **½ teaspoon garlic powder**
- **½ teaspoon salt**
- **Radish slices for garnish**
- **Assorted crudités**

In the bowl of a food processor, combine avocado and lime juice, pulse. Add yogurt, wasabi, garlic powder, salt, pulse till smooth. Cover and chill for 2 hours. Serve with broccoli florets, baby carrots, celery sticks, grape tomatoes, multicolored bell pepper strips, sliced radishes.

Goblin Gourd Ball o' Cheese

Makes 12 or more servings

You want to shred the cheese from a block yourself, do not buy pre-shredded. A block of cheese has kept more of its freshness, fat, and flavor.

> 2 packages (8 ounces each) cream cheese, softened
> 8-ounce block sharp cheddar cheese, shredded (2 cups)
> 8-ounce block pepper jack cheese, shredded (2 cups)
> 4 strips bacon, cooked and chopped fine (about ½ cup)
> 3 scallions, white and green parts, sliced thin
>   (about ½ cup)
> ⅓ cup mayonnaise
> 1 tablespoon Worcestershire sauce
> 1 container (12 ounces) whipped cream cheese spread
> Orange gel food color
> Green gel food color
> 1 large green bell pepper
> Crudités and crackers

In large bowl, combine cream cheese, cheddar, pepper jack, bacon, scallions, mayo, Worcestershire. Stir together well.

Form mixture into a round pumpkin shape with stem on top. Refrigerate, uncovered for one hour. You'll be able to refine your sculpture while it's chilling.

Place three fourths of the whipped cream cheese in a small bowl, add a few drops of orange gel color, stir till you get the color you want. Place remaining fourth in a second bowl and color green.

For face, cut three triangles and a mouth out of green bell pepper, press on "gourd." Chill for another 30 minutes, surround with crackers or crudités and serve.

Marie Laveau's Voodoo Maque Choux

Makes 10 to 12 servings

The Voodoo Queen of New Orleans has a vegetable dish for you.

> ¼ cup (½ stick) butter
> 1 onion, diced
> 3 cloves garlic, minced
> 1 green bell pepper, diced
> 1 red bell pepper, diced
> 3 ribs celery, diced
> 1 bag (24 ounces) frozen corn
> 1 can (15 ounces) blackeyed peas with jalapeños, drained
> 1 can (16 ounces) diced tomatoes
> 1 teaspoon fresh thyme leaves or dried thyme
> 1 cup heavy cream
> 12 large pitted green olives
> 12 pickled spicy green beans (Cajun Chef)
> 1 cup sliced scallions, white and green parts
> Salt and pepper to taste

In a large skillet, over medium-high heat, melt butter.

Cook onion and garlic till softened, 3 minutes. Add peppers and celery, cook another 4 minutes. Add corn, blackeyed peas, tomatoes, thyme, cream. Lower heat to medium and simmer for 25 minutes, partially covered. Meanwhile, place olives on ends of green beans to create voodoo "pins." Stir in scallions, simmer another 3 minutes.

Transfer to serving dish and put green bean and olive "pins" into the maque choux so they are standing upright. Don't fret, sometimes they like to curl over. Laugh quietly to yourself, with an air of mystery, before serving.

Grim Reaper Chopped Salad

Makes 4 to 6 servings

- 1 pound (about 20) shelled and boiled shrimp, tails removed
- 3 cups romaine lettuce in ¾-inch strips
- 1 cup halved grape tomatoes
- 1 cup haricots verts, cooked and cut in 1-inch pieces
- 1 orange bell pepper, diced
- ½ cup finely chopped red onion
- ¾ cup crumbled blue cheese (3 ounces)
- ½ cup fresh basil in thin strips

- ¼ cup red wine vinegar
- 2 tablespoons fresh lemon juice
- 2 teaspoons salt
- Freshly ground pepper
- ¼ cup olive oil

In a large bowl toss shrimp, lettuce, tomatoes, haricots verts, bell pepper, onion, blue cheese, and basil. Whisk together vinegar, lemon juice, salt, pepper to taste, then whisk in oil. Pour dressing around the inner rim of bowl, then toss salad, lightly coating with dressing from bottom of bowl. Chill for 10 minutes and serve.

Wiener Cauldron Double Trouble: Spooky Spuds and Peas That Bubble

Makes 6 servings

One of my most avant-garde recipes. And certainly my longest recipe title. And I couldn't stop eating it! On those chilly autumn nights in October this may indeed become a new family favorite.

12 all beef franks
3 russet potatoes
6 slices bacon
2 small shallots, minced
¼ cup canola oil
2 tablespoons all-purpose flour
2 teaspoons sugar
2 teaspoons salt, divided
¼ cup distilled white vinegar
2 tablespoons butter
2 cans (15 ounces each) sweet peas
1 teaspoon freshly ground pepper
About 8 toothpicks

Cut wieners in half crosswise. Around the inside of a 9-inch pie plate stand wieners on cut ends, forming a ring and leaving space between the outside of the ring and the edge of the plate. Attach together with toothpicks.

Boil potatoes in water to cover, 25 minutes or till tender. When cool enough to handle, peel and cut into bite-size pieces.

In large skillet, cook bacon till slightly browned but not crisp. Remove, leaving fat in pan. Tear or chop cooled bacon into small pieces.

Heat oven to 350°F. In reserved bacon fat over medium heat, sauté shallot till slightly browned, about 4 minutes. To shallot mixture, add the oil over medium heat. Mix in flour, sugar, 1 teaspoon salt, stirring to thoroughly combine. Cook about 4 minutes till mixture thickens and takes on color.

Add potatoes, vinegar, stir till potatoes fully coated, cook till potatoes are browned, about 7 minutes. Remove potatoes and set aside. In same pan, melt butter, add peas, remaining 1 teaspoon salt, pepper, stir.

Spoon potato mixture inside circle of wieners. Cover potatoes completely with peas and encircle outside of franks with remaining peas. Sprinkle crumbled bacon over peas inside the wiener cauldron. Bake uncovered for 25 minutes till heated through. Cackle with sinister glee, warn everyone about the toothpicks, and serve!!

Vampire Loaf of Salmon *(Drac-Snax)*

Makes 4 to 6 servings

This loaf is Dracu-licious!!!

4 large salmon fillets (about 2 pounds)
2 cups panko breadcrumbs
¼ cup finely chopped pimento olives
¼ cup instant diced onion
¼ cup parsley flakes
½ teaspoon red pepper flakes
2 large eggs, lightly beaten
¼ cup heavy cream
2 tablespoons olive oil
1 tablespoon lemon juice
8 ounces bottled cocktail sauce with horseradish
Coarse salt and freshly ground pepper

Heat oven to 350°F. Salt and pepper salmon fillets. Bake 12 to 15 minutes, then flake into large bowl.

To bowl, add bread crumbs, olives, onion, parsley, red pepper, eggs, cream, oil, lemon juice. With hands, mix thoroughly to combine. Line sheet pan with parchment paper or foil and coat with butter or cooking spray. On prepared pan, form salmon mixture into a rectangular "neck"-shaped loaf.

Bake uncovered for 40 minutes. Using two wide spatulas, transfer loaf to serving platter. Decorate salmon "neck" with "streams of blood" (cocktail sauce). Serve immediately, while haunting organ music plays.

Ghoul Fuel Spectral Spinach

Makes 6 servings

A side course of supernatural energy!

- ½ cup (1 stick) butter, divided
- 2 teaspoons salt, divided
- 2 pounds crinkly Savoy spinach, remove stems (This might take a little while . . . a project for the kids?)
- ½ cup chicken or vegetable broth
- 2 tablespoons flour
- ¼ cup instant diced onion, or ½ shallot, minced
- ½ teaspoon garlic powder
- ½ teaspoon nutmeg
- 1 teaspoon coarsely ground pepper
- 6 ounces pepper jack cheese, in small cubes
- 2 jars (4 ounces each) sliced sweet pimentos, drained

In large high-sided skillet, over medium heat, melt half a stick butter with 1 teaspoon salt. Wilt half the spinach (about 4 minutes) but let it keep some of its spring. Repeat with remaining half stick butter, 1 teaspoon salt and second half spinach. Collect spinach without it's "liquor" in a large bowl to the side.

Get ready to stir: to skillet over medium heat add broth, flour, onions, garlic powder, nutmeg, pepper. Stir briefly till smooth and thick. Add spinach, stir. Add cheese and melt. Throw in pimentos, coat all with sauce. Stir together for 5 to 7 minutes to fully heat spinach.

Bayou Stew for the Rougarou
aka *Chicken Andouille Gumbo*

Makes 6 to 8 servings

This classic stew, or gumbo, is sure to protect you from the legendary Cajun wolfman swamp-monster known as the Rougarou. He can't count past twelve, so this stew has over thirteen tasty ingredients. Try to count those, you Rougarou! The Rou' loves raw meat, but we're cooking ours, so that should send him packing as well. Some say you should put a leaf from the swamp in your pocket to ward him off. We have two bay leaves to take care of that (one for you and one for a friend).

As the legend goes, if you've been a bad kid, or if you haven't observed Lent seven years in a row, you might turn into a Rougarou. No matter how you've sinned, making this chicken andouille stew is sure to keep the monster at bay!

4 bone-in chicken breasts

Salt and freshly ground pepper

12 ounces andouille sausage, cut in ½-inch slices

⅓ cup canola oil

½ cup all-purpose flour

2 large cloves garlic, minced

1 medium sweet onion, chopped fine

4 ribs celery, chopped fine

1 large green bell pepper, chopped fine

2 quarts hot water

1 tablespoon Worcestershire sauce

2 bay leaves

Heaping ⅓ cup chopped parsley

2 teaspoons gumbo filé

Season chicken generously with salt and pepper.

In a big (7.25 quart) Dutch oven over medium-high heat, add andouille and fry for several minutes, set aside. Add chicken and cook till browned on all sides, about 6 minutes each batch, set aside.

To make the Rou'-stew-roux: reduce heat to medium-low, add the oil, add the flour. Stir constantly till mixture becomes a thick golden brown, 8 to 12 minutes.

Add garlic, onion, celery, bell pepper. Cook, stirring, till vegetables soften, about 5 minutes. Add the water. Add Worcestershire sauce, bay leaves, chicken, reduce to a simmer. Cover and stir occasionally, 1 hour.

Remove chicken, shred meat off the bone in bite-size pieces, return meat to pot, discard bones. Remove bay leaves (don't worry, they're still protecting you). Stir in parsley and andouille. Turn off heat and let sit for 30 minutes. To serve, re-heat to a simmer and stir in the filé.

Now, relax! Serve over rice with your favorite hot sauce close at hand. The Rougarou can't get you!

183

Thrilling Chilling Chocolate Spider Pie

4 cups graham cracker crumbs (about 24 four-cracker sheets), finely ground in food processor
6 tablespoons sugar
1 teaspoon salt
3 tablespoons unsalted butter, melted, and more for greasing
3 tablespoons creamy peanut butter (Skippy preferred)
5 tablespoons cool water

16 ounces good quality semi-sweet chocolate, chopped
3 tablespoons sugar
2 cups heavy cream
¾ cup (1 ½ sticks) butter cut into cubes, slightly softened

¼ cup sweetened condensed milk
⅓ cup creamy peanut butter (Skippy preferred)
2 tablespoons butter, softened

Generously butter a deep 9 ½-inch pie plate. To a medium bowl add crumbs, sugar, salt, whisk together. Add 3 tablespoons butter, 3 tablespoons peanut butter, water. With hand, thoroughly combine till crust is like wet sand. With hand press into pie plate. Make crust approximately ¼-inch thick. Crust should come up sides of the plate and finish smoothly. Refrigerate uncovered 30 minutes.

When crust is ready, add chocolate and sugar to medium bowl. In small pot over medium heat bring heavy cream just to a bubbling simmer, then pour cream over chocolate, wait 2 minutes. Stir chocolate and cream together thoroughly using a circular motion. As you stir, watch for the moment of truth when the white of the cream suddenly changes to glossy brown. Add butter and stir in with spoon till blended; make sure no lumps of butter remain. Pour ganache into crust. Set aside for a moment while you prepare peanut butter ganache.

In a small pot over medium low heat, place condensed milk, ⅓ cup peanut butter, 2 tablespoons softened butter. Let sit over heat for 1 minute to warm milk. Stir till just combined. Pour mixture into a 1 quart resealable plastic storage bag and snip off the tiniest corner. And I mean tiny. You can always make it bigger if needed. Squeeze some out on a nearby plate to get the hang of it. Beginning in center of the pie, pipe a tight spiral of peanut butter mixture, working outwards. To create web, with a toothpick, draw lines through the rings of the spiral both from the center towards the edge, and from the edge towards the center. Voila, web. Now all you need is the spider.

Place pie carefully in fridge. Chill, uncovered while filling sets, 3 to 4 hours or overnight. Keep pie in fridge between servings.

Pro Tip: Let pie sit out of fridge for 15 minutes before serving for best texture and flavor.

Midnight Cake with Molten Orange Frosting

Devil's food cake and eerie orange molten frosting with festive Mellowcreme pumpkin toppers!

CAKE
2 cups unbleached all-purpose flour
1 teaspoon salt
2 teaspoon baking soda
1 teaspoon baking powder
1 teaspoon cornstarch
¾ cup unsweetened cocoa powder
1 cup packed light brown sugar
1 cup white sugar
1 cup canola oil
1 teaspoon vanilla
3 large eggs
1 ½ cups whole milk
¼ cup mayonnaise

FROSTING
1 stick butter, softened
5 cups confectioners' sugar, divided (a 1 pound box
    contains about 3 ½ cups)
¼ cup and 2 tablespoons milk, divided
1 teaspoon vanilla
2 tablespoons grated orange zest
¼ cup orange juice
Orange gel food coloring (preferable to common
    liquid coloring)
½ cup unsweetened cocoa powder
9 Mellowcreme pumpkins for decoration

For cake: Heat oven to 350°F. Butter and flour two 8-inch round pans.

In medium bowl, whisk together flour, salt, baking soda, baking powder, cornstarch, and cocoa. In a large bowl, beat together sugars, oil, and vanilla. Add eggs to sugar mixture one at a time. Next, alternating between them in thirds, beat flour mixture and milk into sugar and egg mixture.

Pour batter into pans and bake 35 to 45 minutes or till a toothpick comes out clean. Turn cake layers out of pans and cool. They may be a little sticky but that's okay.

For frosting: In a large bowl, beat together butter, sugar, milk, vanilla. Divide ¾ and ¼ between two bowls. For the first ¾ frosting, to frost whole cake, stir in orange zest, orange juice, and food coloring. Spread some between the two layers, stopping just inside the edge of layers, then flood the top of cake and let the rest run down sides. You can help the "flooding" across the top with a spatula. It's okay to have areas of the bottom cake layer not covered by frosting, that's part of the effect. Frosting should harden like molten Halloween lava! For chocolate rosettes: add ½ cup cocoa and 2 tablespoons milk to the other ¼ frosting and pipe nine rosettes on top of cake. Place one of the nine Mellowcreme pumpkins in the center of each!

Mock Turtle Soup *(Turtle in Costume)*

Makes 4 to 6 servings

Turtle soup is a dish that enjoys vast popularity in New Orleans. It is a classic starter at more than one legendary local establishment. If you have no turtle meat on hand though, what do you do? This recipe is your answer. One can only hope to be in the same number as JoAnn Clevenger's heavenly Upperline turtle soup (see her story, next page) when the turtles, er, saints, go marchin' in.

1 tablespoon and ⅓ cup canola oil, divided

2 pounds beef chuck for stew, cut in 1-inch pieces

½ cup all-purpose flour

2 cloves garlic, minced

1 medium red onion, diced

3 ribs celery, diced

1 medium green bell pepper, diced

2 cups beef broth

2 cups chicken broth

1 can (14.5 ounces) diced tomatoes

½ teaspoon cayenne pepper

2 bay leaves

1 teaspoon salt

4 chopped hard boiled eggs

1 ½ tablespoons fresh lemon juice

Sherry for serving

NATIONAL CAT DAY:
OCTOBER
29

In large Dutch oven or heavy pot, heat 1 tablespoon oil over medium-high heat. In batches, cook meat till browned well on all sides. Set meat aside. Reduce heat to medium-low, add ⅓ cup oil to pot, with wooden spoon scrape up the fond/brown bits/gradoux. After one minute mix in flour. Making small circles, stir constantly to keep roux from sticking or burning. Cook till is a dark caramel color. This will take 20 to 30 minutes so put on some good music!

When roux is ready, add garlic, stir for 30 seconds, then add the trinity (onion, celery, bell pepper). Mix to combine roux with vegetables, about 30 seconds, creating a sticky paste. Add both broths, the tomatoes, cayenne, bay leaves. Simmer for 45 minutes partially covered, stirring frequently. Sprinkle 1 teaspoon of salt over the chopped eggs. Add eggs and lemon juice to soup. Simmer another 15 minutes. Remove bay leaves. Add a splash of sherry to each serving as preferred.

Dateline: New Orleans. In the most haunted room of the Monteleone Hotel, I bravely consulted the spirited JoAnn Clevenger, owner and celebrated host of Upperline Restaurant, on what it takes to forever serve uncanny food, and what she does to seem practically supernatural while doing it.

A special group of Crescent City luminaries from various artistic callings was also on hand to enjoy bowls of Upperline's acclaimed turtle soup and of course, a Sazerac, or three. The child ghost known to haunt the famous room, Maurice Begere, did not partake, but he was there in spirit.

Flavor, flavor, flavor.

I will read from my list of 13 questions, because we're on the 13th floor, and it's a Halloween party. Southern Living *says you have the best front-of-house hospitality in the region. What makes someone a great host, whether professionally or at home?*

Loving, kindness, graciousness, and knowledge. The original meaning of restaurant is restorative, and that's my goal. The guest leaves and feels self-enhanced. They feel braver and stronger and more patient and kind, and what I like to tell myself, silly. I think it's important to not be too formal to have that sense of whimsy and silly.

Upperline's turtle soup, which we've all just enjoyed in this room, which is a thrill—I must admit

this party is a dream of mine come true—is one of the truly great turtle soups in town. What do you think makes it better than the rest?

Exotic. We keep the ingredients from the 19th century, which have been filtered out over the years. There's an Americanized turtle soup you find quite often. It's good, but not exotic. The flavorings of the 18th and 19th century, they used cloves and allspice and lemons. Then we keep all the usual Creole thyme, bay leaf, red pepper flakes. We slice lemons and add them to ours because of the acid from the pulp and the zest from the peel. You have different layers of flavor, which is what I'm always seeking.

If you had to choose a single reason why people like

188

the food you serve, what would it be?

Flavor, flavor, flavor. Along with flavor, you have to have good execution. You can't get good flavor unless someone knows what they're doing when they sauté or braise or broil or grill. Along with flavor is the mouth feel. With Creole food it's contrast and texture, the way it affects your mouth.

What is your favorite dish at Upperline and why?

The Sundae Eugene, which is vanilla ice cream with our semi-sweet warm chocolate sauce—which has a tiny bit too much salt. So that tiny bit of extra salt is colliding with that extra sweet creaminess, and it creates a dramatic tension. And you crave that next bite. That's what people really get excited about.

There is a wonderful short film on the internet that calls you "a Girl Scout with gumption." What advice would you give the home cook or host that might help them have more gumption like you do?

Don't give up. Don't give up. Be prepared. And that's the reason I wear my Girl Scout pin, to be prepared for those unforeseen events that put a damper on whatever you're trying to achieve. Don't give up. And realize that what you're doing, being brave, strong, patient, kind, can make a difference, not just to my life but to the lives of the people in the restaurant that work there and the lives of the people that come there to have dinner and the lives of the post-

man and the delivery people. You can make a difference in other people's lives by just having a tiny bit of empathy and kindness even when you goof up. And we all goof up. Being able to say, "I'm so sorry I goofed. I didn't mean to." Being willing to fail, because we do fail. I wish I didn't, but I do.

At the end of a dinner at Upperline, besides your customers telling you personally, are there any unspoken signs or signals that tell you you've done a great job as host and restaurateur?

They don't want to leave. They stand up, but they sort of look at all the other people, and they still want to be part of the scene. I think that breaking bread with strangers in a dining room, we're different from each other, can show more acceptance of the fact that we're all one. We're seeing the differences, yet we're all enjoying the same food. We all use a napkin and love the Sundae Eugene, so we share humanity with each other. And I can tell by their posture, it's a subtle thing. Then they come up to the maître d' stand, or they wait by the door while I'm seating some other guest, "I just wanted to tell you how much–" but first, they want to touch me. They give me a hug. Sometimes I'll reach out my hand to shake theirs, "Oh, no. Not a shake. No shaking here. I want to hug you." Those hugs, they don't say how much they enjoyed. They just hug me, and it's so meaningful.

Thanksgiving Bons Temps Rouler

Plateau de Relish Maison with Trempette au Roquefort

Good for a party of 12

In my research on Thanksgiving and other event menus from the past two centuries I've encountered frequent starter relish courses of stuffed celery, olives, pickles, and almonds. I had the idea of a sort of chic plateau (tray) with a luscious blue cheese dip as a "new" tradition to start off the big meal. It has proven to be a big hit at every type of party!

8 ounces blue cheese

8 ounces cream cheese

½ cup mayonnaise

1 clove garlic, minced

2 tablespoons red wine vinegar

2 teaspoons sugar

Couple dashes hot sauce

2 tablespoons finely chopped parsley

Crudités, olives, nuts, cornichons

In a medium-sized bowl, using a large spoon, combine all ingredients thoroughly, but don't purée. The dip should still be chunky. Refrigerate, covered, for at least 3 hours before serving, preferably overnight. Serve, using your most breathtaking platter or snack set, with vegetable crudités: carrot and celery sticks, colorful sliced bell peppers, radishes, pimento-stuffed olives. Cornichons (French gherkins) are especially delicious with this dip! Throw in some salted or smoked almonds for extra credit.

Turkey Tactics

Plan ahead: for a whole or partial frozen bird, defrost in fridge one day for every 3.5 to 4 pounds of turkey.

Bons Temps Roulade of Turkey with Rosemary-Sausage Stuffing

Makes 8 servings. DELICIOUS.

- 4 tablespoons butter (½ stick), plus more to brush exterior
- 1 medium sweet onion, chopped fine (1 ½ cups)
- 3 large ribs celery, chopped fine (1 ¼ cups)
- 2 large carrots, chopped fine (1 ½ cups)
- 2 large cloves garlic, minced
- 1 pound sweet Italian sausage, casings removed
- ½ cup chopped pimento-stuffed olives (about 8 jumbo stuffed olives)
- 2 tablespoons chopped fresh rosemary leaves
- 3 cups stuffing mix (like Pepperidge Farm Herb Seasoned)
- 1 teaspoon dried oregano
- 3 tablespoons distilled white vinegar
- 1 large egg
- ¾ cup chicken broth
- 5 pound skin-on turkey breast, boned, butterflied
- Salt and freshly ground pepper

In a large skillet over medium heat melt ¼ cup butter. Add onion, celery, carrots, and garlic and cook 5 to 6 minutes till vegetables begin to soften. Add sausage, season lightly with salt and pepper. Break it up and cook till no longer pink, about 7 minutes. Add olives and sprinkle in rosemary, cook another 2 minutes. Transfer vegetable-sausage mixture to large bowl. Add stuffing mix to bowl. Season with oregano, vinegar. Add egg and broth. Stir together well.

Heat oven to 350°F. Spray a roasting pan with cooking spray.

On a cutting board, lay butterflied breast skin side down. Cover with plastic wrap or wax paper, pound with smooth side of meat mallet to an even thickness, as thin as you can get it. You will end up with a rough rectangle with long and short sides. Flip breast so is skin side down, lightly salt and pepper.

On a large cutting board or other non-slip surface, position breast so one of the short sides is closest to you. Cut about 6 14-inch long pieces of kitchen twine and lay them parallel to the long sides, underneath the turkey breast. Place about 2 cups of stuffing in a cylindrical shape on the edge of the short side closest to you and slowly roll it up inside the breast to form a log that is even in diameter, making sure stuffing doesn't smoosh out the ends as you roll. With the twine you placed under the turkey, securely tie roast crosswise every few inches. Cut another long piece of twine and tie one more time longwise to keep ends secure. Place rolled breast seam side down in roasting pan. Brush with 1 tablespoon melted butter and season liberally with salt and pepper. Roast roulade uncovered for about 1 hour 40 minutes till you reach an internal temperature of 160°F to 165°F. Thirty minutes before roasting time is up, surround with remaining stuffing to brown.

Insert thermometer in more than one spot to confirm temperature. Roulade will rise by at least five degrees as it rests. Tent with foil, rest for 15 minutes, remove twine, and carve. Serve with the additional stuffing.

Creole Crawfish 'n Cornbread Dressing

Makes 4 to 6 servings

This crawfish, andouille, and cornbread dressing is great with a lot of mains besides turkey, all year long. I love it with a big broiled pork chop and buttery petits pois. The pickled vegetables add a tangy Sicilian touch. The slicing and dicing for this recipe is well worth it. It's enjoyable to put together. You can make the day before and cover tightly in fridge. It stays tasty and moist. Reheat, covered, at 325°F for 45 minutes.

7 cups Belle Reve Honey Cornbread (recipe this chapter), ½ to ¾-inch cubes. Uses about ⅔ of the cornbread, so you have some left to warm up and serve with the meal.

12 ounces andouille sausage, diced

¼ cup (½ stick) butter

1 small sweet onion, diced (about 1 cup)

2 ribs celery, sliced thin

1 small green bell pepper, diced

2 bay leaves

1 teaspoon dried oregano

1 teaspoon garlic powder

1 pound crawfish tails, thawed and patted dry

2 teaspoons Creole seasoning with salt (like Tony Chachere's)

½ teaspoon freshly ground pepper

⅔ cup muffuletta salad or chopped mild giardiniera

½ cup chopped flat leaf parsley

1 cup sliced scallions, mostly white, some green parts

1 large egg, lightly beaten

2 cups chicken broth (with salt)

Make Belle Reve Honey Cornbread (page 197), let sit for an hour then cube. Heat oven to 350°F. Grease a 9x13-inch baking dish with butter. On a baking sheet, spread the cornbread cubes, toast in oven 15 minutes, set aside.

In a Dutch oven or large pot, heat sausage over medium to medium-high heat, about 4 minutes, push sausage to the side of the pot. Melt butter in pot. Add onion, celery, bell peppers, bay leaves, oregano, and garlic powder. Cook vegetables till softened, about 8 minutes.

Add crawfish, Creole seasoning, pepper. Toss with vegetables till just heated, 4 minutes. Remove bay leaves and reduce heat to low.

In a very large bowl, whisk together muffuletta salad, parsley, scallions, egg, broth. Fold in the cornbread, and the andouille/crawfish mixture. Combine gently but thoroughly.

To prepared baking dish, add dressing mixture. Bake uncovered till bubbling, about 30 minutes.

Sweet Potatoes Irma

Makes 8 servings

I named this dish after Irma Thomas, "The Soul Queen of New Orleans," because it has a whole lot of spirit and a tender touch of sweet.

- **3 tablespoons butter, divided**
- **1 small onion, diced fine**
- **2 cloves garlic, minced**
- **2 tablespoons fresh rosemary leaves, chopped fine**
- **2 tablespoons brown sugar**
- **½ teaspoon nutmeg**
- **1 pint heavy cream (2 cups)**
- **½ cup vegetable broth**
- **3 large russet potatoes, sliced thin (do this when you need them so they don't go brown on you)**
- **3 large sweet potatoes, sliced thin**
- **¾ cup shredded Parmesan**
- **1 ¼ cup shredded Gruyère (about ⅓ pound)**
- **Salt and freshly ground pepper**

Heat oven to 350°F. Grease a 13 x 9-inch baking dish with one tablespoon butter.

In a medium skillet over medium heat, melt two tablespoons butter. Add onion and garlic, cook till softened, 4 minutes. Add rosemary, brown sugar, nutmeg, cream, broth, ½ teaspoon each salt and pepper. Heat just to a boil, remove from heat.

Add a bit of cream mixture to dish. Over this, start with a single layer of potatoes then a single layer of sweet potatoes, then a layer of both cheeses, then a layer of cream mixture. Repeat, till you're all used up, making sure to end with a topping of cheese. Cover with foil and bake 1 hour or till potatoes are soft. Uncover for last 15 minutes of baking.

Shrimp-Stuffed Mirlitons

Makes 8 servings

A New Orleans classic.

- **8 medium mirlitons**
- **1 ½ sticks butter, divided**
- **1 sweet onion, diced**
- **2 ribs celery, diced**
- **1 red bell pepper, diced**
- **1 green bell pepper, diced**
- **2 cloves garlic, minced**
- **1 teaspoon salt**
- **Juice of 1 lemon**
- **2 teaspoons celery seed**
- **Couple dashes of your favorite hot sauce**
- **2 pounds medium shrimp, peeled and chopped**
- **2 cups French bread torn in bite sized chunks**
- **¾ cup panko breadcrumbs**

In large pot, cover mirlitons with water 1 or 2 inches above. Boil 45 minutes or till fork tender. Slice in half lengthwise, remove and discard seeds. Scoop out flesh leaving ½-inch thick "shells." Reserve flesh. Invert shells to drain on paper towels or wire rack.

Heat oven to 350°F. In large skillet or Dutch oven melt 1 stick butter over med high heat, add trinity (onion, celery, bell peppers), garlic, season with salt, cook 8 minutes till softened. Add lemon juice, celery seed, hot sauce, shrimp. Cook till shrimp are pink. In large bowl, combine shrimp mixture with mirliton pulp, fold in French bread.

Set mirliton shells side by side in aluminum or other roasting pan. Stuff shells with shrimp and bread mixture. In small saucepan melt remaining ½ stick butter, stir in panko crumbs. Top stuffed mirlitons with buttered crumbs. Bake 25 minutes uncovered.

Italian Green Bean Casserole

Makes 6 servings

With all admiration for the renowned Dorcas Reilly, who, in 1955, invented the ubiquitous, beloved, Campbell's Soup green bean casserole with crunchy onions, I present my exotic international alternative, in case you ever want to startle and delight the ones you love. Frozen Italian green beans will also work, but I prefer canned. I'm sure Ms. Reilly would approve. I also serve this dish as individual sides, per the photo.

2 tablespoons extra virgin olive oil
1 small onion, diced
2 cloves garlic, minced
8 ounces fresh white mushrooms, sliced

½ cup fresh basil chopped
3 tablespoons red wine vinegar
½ teaspoon dried oregano
½ teaspoon sugar
10 ounces grape tomatoes, sliced in half
2 cans (14 ounces each) Italian cut green beans, drained
½ cup shredded Parmesan
½ cup panko breadcrumbs
1 cup shredded mozzarella
Salt and pepper to taste

Heat oven to 350°F. Grease or spray an 8 x 8-inch baking dish.

In large skillet with high sides, heat oil over medium heat. Cook onion and garlic till softened, about 4 minutes. Add mushrooms, basil, vinegar, oregano, sugar, stir, cooking another 2 minutes. Add tomatoes, cook till they begin to wilt slightly and mushrooms cook down a bit, about 7 minutes.

In medium bowl, toss together green beans, Parmesan, panko.

To baking dish add one half bean mixture, a modest shake of salt and pepper, top with a layer of tomato mixture, then half the mozzarella. Repeat with other half bean mixture, salt and pepper, rest of tomato mixture, rest of mozzarella.

Bake, covered, for 25 minutes till heated through and cheese topping has melted.

Haricots Verts Extraordinaires

Makes 6 to 8 servings

1 ½ pounds haricots verts, stem ends trimmed
6 tablespoons butter
⅓ cup finely chopped red onion
1 tablespoon fresh thyme leaves

½ teaspoon ground nutmeg
Juice of one lemon
Salt and freshly ground pepper

Boil a large pot of water, add a generous amount of salt. Add beans and cook for 7 minutes. To stop cooking and enhance color, plunge beans into large bowl of ice water. Drain well and set aside.

In large skillet, over medium heat, melt butter and cook, whisking constantly, till it turns light brown. Immediately add red onion, thyme, nutmeg, and lemon juice. Add beans to skillet, stir thoroughly.

Season to taste with salt and pepper, serve immediately.

Belle Reve Honey Cornbread

Makes 12 servings

Just like Blanche used to bake. Comes together quick. Fun to make, simply delicious. Infinitely better than a mix.

1 ⅓ cup unbleached all-purpose flour
⅔ cup yellow cornmeal
¼ cup brown sugar, packed
1 tablespoon baking powder
1 teaspoon arrowroot starch or cornstarch
1 teaspoon salt
1 ¼ cup milk
½ cup honey
¼ cup (½ stick) unsalted butter, very soft,
    more to grease pan
¼ cup canola oil
2 large eggs

Heat oven to 375°F. Grease a 9 x 9-inch baking pan.

In a large bowl, whisk together flour, cornmeal, sugar, baking powder, starch, salt.

In medium bowl, whisk together milk, honey, butter, oil, eggs. With wooden spoon, stir liquid mixture into dry, combining thoroughly to make a smooth batter. It is okay if you still have some chunks of butter. Pour into prepared pan. Bake for 22 to 25 minutes till a toothpick comes out clean.

Cool for 15 minutes and slice into portions as preferred.

Apple Pandowdy

Makes 8 servings

Shoo fly pie, and apple pan dowdy
Makes your eyes light up, your tummy say "Howdy."
   —*Sammy Gallop, 1945*

Bons Temps Rouler, the Northeastern way. Almost more tart than sweet, it cries out for a huge scoop of vanilla ice cream on top. A bit of effort goes into this one but if you follow the recipe carefully you will create a masterpiece of YUM. I make this in a 9-inch metal pie pan. After all, it's a pan-dowdy. The metal is also a bit better at cooking the bottom crust compared to glass.

CRUST

2 ½ cups unbleached all-purpose flour

1 teaspoon salt

¼ cup lard, or vegetable shortening

10 tablespoons chilled butter, cut in small cubes

Ice water

FILLING

3 pounds Granny Smith apples peeled, cored, sliced in bite-size chunks (5 to 8 apples depending on size. Keep in bowl of water as you work on them to avoid browning.)

6 tablespoons butter

½ cup light brown sugar, packed

2 teaspoons cinnamon

1 teaspoon nutmeg

½ teaspoon salt

2 tablespoons lemon juice

1 tablespoon vanilla extract

1 ½ tablespoons apple cider vinegar

1 tablespoon arrowroot starch or cornstarch

2 tablespoons molasses

1 egg, lightly beaten

1 tablespoon granulated sugar

In large bowl, whisk together flour and salt. With fingers, break up lard or shortening into small pieces, work thoroughly into flour till sandy. Work chilled cubed butter in to flour mixture till just combined. Add 4 tablespoons and two teaspoons ice water as needed, knead together to form dough. Don't overdo it or you will lose flakiness. Divide and make two disks, one about 2 thirds of the dough and the other about 1 third, wrap in plastic, refrigerate at least 30 minutes.

Heat oven to 425°F. Butter a 9-inch metal pie pan.

Drain and dry apples with paper towels if you've held them in water. Working quickly, in a large deep skillet, over medium-high heat, melt 6 tablespoons butter. Add brown sugar, cinnamon, nutmeg, salt, mix to combine. Add apples, lemon juice, vanilla, stir. Whisk together apple cider vinegar and starch and add. Cook over medium heat, stirring occasionally, for 12 to 15 minutes till apples have softened but are not mushy. Set aside to cool.

Roll out larger portion of crust for bottom of pie to about ¼-inch thick, cover bottom of pan and up the sides ending a bit over the edge. It helps to roll out between two sheets of parchment paper, with a rolling pin. It's okay if the edges look "rustic."

Pour in apple filling. If there is too much liquid, remove with soup spoon. Mixture should, however, still have a lot of the pan juices remaining. Drizzle with the molasses. Roll out remaining dough to ¼-inch and cover, sealing by folding edge of the bottom crust over the edge of the top (or just smoosh them together well). Whisk the egg together with a tablespoon of water and brush top (or spread on with your fingers if you don't have a brush handy). Sprinkle egg wash with the granulated sugar. Place on a cookie sheet to catch any overflow and bake till puffed and nicely set, 15 minutes.

Reduce heat to 350°F.

With a paring knife, slice top crust into 1 to 2 inch squares and push down into filling a bit. This is your chance to do an awesome art project. It's called "dowdying!"

Bake 25 minutes more till filling is done and crust edges are tinged with gold. Rest at least one hour so the pandowdy can fully find itself, then serve.

Napkin Folding

THE PYRAMID

Using a square napkin, folding away from you, bring one corner to touch the opposite corner to make a triangle.

Bring the left and right corners to the top, creating a square.

Carefully flip napkin over so it's oriented the same way, just upside-down.

Fold it in the middle away from you to make a smaller triangle.

Spin the triangle around 180°.

Fold the sides downward and away from you, and voila!

THE GOBLET FAN

Fold napkin in half to form a rectangle, with one short end nearest you.

Make 1 ½-inch pleated accordion folds starting at one short end and ending at the other.

Fold the hemmed end over 2-inches towards the center.

Place end in the nearest goblet and fan it out!

Galatoire's—The James Beard Award-winning Outstanding Restaurant in America.

Chef Phillip Lopez, one of the most celebrated chefs of the avant-garde in New Orleans, takes the helm at one of the most historic bastions of New Orleans cuisine, and is dedicated to upholding the old traditions. His admiration is for the culinary legacy of the city. And our admiration is for him.

Because of the food

I wanted to talk to you about Thanksgiving because my Thanksgiving chapter has a lot of New Orleans dishes. Something people should know about you is you're very experienced in molecular gastronomy. How do you feel a home cook would be influenced by that, or would they?

Well a good label for molecular gastronomy could be modern cuisine. At the same time, just boiling water can be considered molecular gastronomy. And for a home cook to start thinking about modern cuisine and how to be a better home cook, the first thing they would need to realize is that they need to have really good salt. Regular iodized table salt is a flavor masker, so it doesn't produce a pure result. You want a really good kosher salt, it's the best type for the home cook to use.

You have a lot of global culinary experience. You've lived in Germany, France, Spain, Austria.

And we traveled through Asia. Japan, Shanghai, Hong Kong, Vietnam. I was influenced as a young child by all these travels. I had the opportunity to be exposed to a lot of different cuisines and flavors and spices that, believe it or not, all exist here in New Orleans. They just get overshadowed by the Creole spice and the Cajun.

What's your favorite Thanksgiving dish, and why?

There are so many that I can name. But if I was to pick one, it would have to be the turkey because it is the easiest thing to mess up, and then when it's done right it is oh so good. Down here in the South, we tend to fry a lot of the turkeys. I grew up in a household where it was always in the oven slow and low. It baked. It started off early in the morning. And so the crispy skin, the moist meat. Then the combination of things that you can make after the dinner always excited me, the opportunities to do turkey salad or make a really good turkey soup. Turkey is much more flexible than, say, potato salad, which you can't really transform.

You can't even do a potato salad sandwich, can you?

You CAN just throw it in a pot of gumbo.

Ha ha, exactly! Throw it in the gumbo. Do you tend to be creative and try new things every year for Thanksgiving? Or do you just kind of stick with what you know everyone will like?

No, I definitely change it up over the years. Some years I would pack underneath the skin a lot of herbs and butter. One year, I brined the turkey in vanilla and bourbon.

Mmm! Speaking of creative, have you ever served an unexpected dish at Thanksgiving and everyone went, "Whoa!" Something that no one expects?

Last year, I got the itch to do a prime rib. So I got a big one, bone-in, covered it with herbs and garlic and olive oil and slow roasted in the oven.

You did a turkey as well, or–

A turkey as well, yeah.

Wow, that's definitely an ambitious unexpected dish. So, how would you improve a Thanksgiving staple? Like the tried and true green bean casserole from the Campbell's Soup lady from 1955. How would you make that better? Or do you think it's perfect already?

For me, the green bean casserole is one of those things where you sit down and if it's not on the plate with your turkey dinner, you're asking questions.

Is there anything else that you would add for the home cook reader?

Don't be scared of cooking. I think, as a society, we've gotten away from sitting at the dinner table. We've gotten away from being in the kitchen cooking. Everything's become so fast-paced. For me, the reason why I'm so passionate about food and so passionate about not only the exploration of food and techniques but also the ability to preserve the history as well at the same time, has been because I grew up in a family for whom turning off the TV, setting the table, and sitting down as a family was very important. It was the time that we talked about our problems. We talked about the things that we wanted to accomplish. And we were able to resolve things at the same time. And it was because of the food. It gave us an opportunity to break down the barriers.

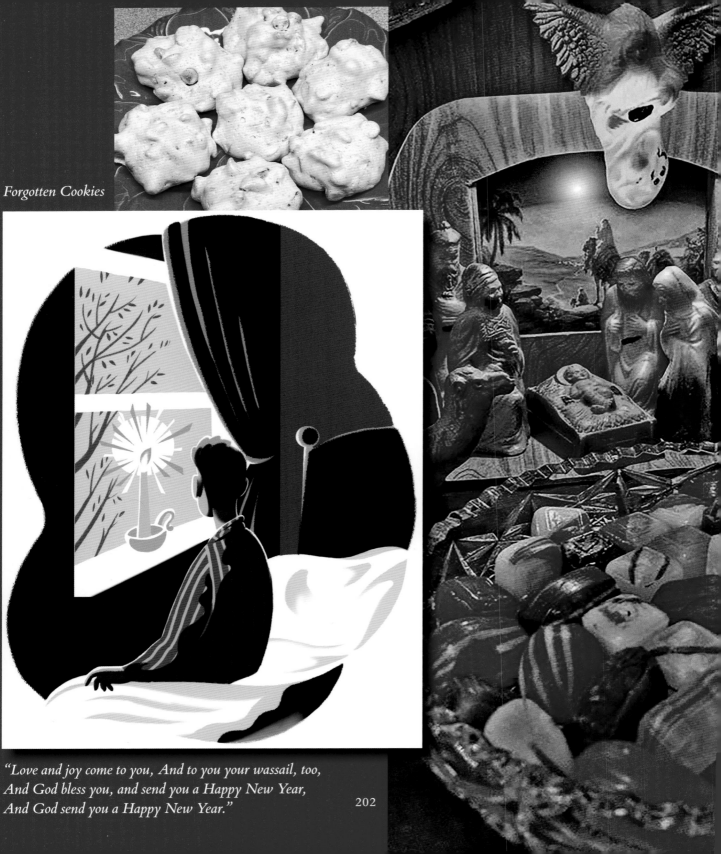

Forgotten Cookies

"*Love and joy come to you, And to you your wassail, too,
And God bless you, and send you a Happy New Year,
And God send you a Happy New Year.*"

SILVER BELLS

Carolers' Wassail Punch

Makes 8 cups, 12 servings

- 1 navel orange
- 16 whole cloves
- 2 quarts fresh apple cider
- 1 quart cranberry juice cocktail
- 1 cup orange juice
- ⅓ cup honey

- 2 three-inch cinnamon sticks
- 6 whole allspice berries
- 12 black peppercorns

Insert cloves into orange in a festive pattern. In large pot, combine cider, cranberry juice, orange juice, honey. Tie cinnamon sticks, allspice, and peppercorns in cheesecloth, add to pot. Bring wassail almost to a boil. Reduce heat and simmer 5 minutes. Remove cheesecloth sachet. Present the wassail in your best punch bowl with ladle, floating the orange for decoration, or serve in mugs.

Forgotten Cookies

Makes 24 to 28 cookies

The magical snowy cookies of my childhood.

- 2 large egg whites, at room temperature - important
- ⅔ cup sugar
- ½ teaspoon salt

- 1 teaspoon vanilla extract
- 1 cup chopped pecans
- 1 cup semi-sweet chocolate chips

Heat oven to 350°F. In large bowl, beat egg whites till soft peaks form, then very gradually add the sugar, beating constantly till fairly stiff peaks form. Into the egg mixture gently fold pecans, chocolate chips, vanilla, salt, till evenly distributed. Don't overmix.

Line cookie sheets with parchment paper. Drop mixture by the heaping tablespoonful. They don't spread much so you can space them 1 inch apart. Place cookie sheets side by side on center rack of oven, or stagger on two racks so one is not above the other. Turn off oven right away. Then forget about them! By tomorrow morning they will be done.

Christmas Party Meatballs

Makes 50 meatballs

A mid-century classic and my Mother-in-Law's specialty. These are more sweet 'n sour-ly hard to resist than ever. I normally make 300 meatballs for 100 people. Be sure to take meatballs out of freezer the day before, to thaw in fridge.

⅓ cup all fruit grape jelly

½ cup chili sauce

2 tablespoons soy sauce

1 tablespoon brown sugar

¼ cup apple cider vinegar

1 tablespoon arrowroot starch or cornstarch

50 frozen plain or Swedish meatballs, thawed. Do not use Italian-flavored.

In Dutch oven or large pot combine jelly, chili sauce, soy sauce, sugar, vinegar. Over medium heat, whisk vigorously and bring to a gentle boil. Add 1 ½ tablespoons water to starch, whisk, stir in to mixture. Continue cooking till mixture thickens, about 4 minutes. Add meatballs. With large spoon coat meatballs with sauce by turning them repeatedly, 5 minutes. Simmer for another 10, stirring frequently to avoid scorching. Refrigerate meatballs in sauce for at least 3 hours, best overnight. In foil-covered roasting pan, at 225°F, reheat for 45 minutes then hold in oven at 225°F till ready to serve.

Insalata Russa

Makes 8 to 12 servings

This is a part of the Feast of the Seven Fishes, beginning next page

If I had to choose five goodwill recipes of mine from this book to put on a silicon disc to send to the moon on the next manned spaceflight, this would be one of them. The international potato salad that just goes with everything.

2 large russet potatoes

1 cup carrots, cut in ¼-inch dice

¼ cup sliced pimento-stuffed olives

3 tablespoons capers

3 tablespoons olive oil

2 tablespoons red wine vinegar

½ teaspoon salt

1 teaspoon freshly ground pepper

¾ cup mayonnaise

In medium pot cover potatoes with cold water, bring to boil. Reduce heat, simmer uncovered 20 minutes. Add carrots to pot. Cook till potatoes still firm but knife inserted in potato goes through easily (this is important), about 10 minutes. Drain all in colander, set under cold running water for 2 minutes.

Peel potatoes, cut into ½-inch cubes. In large bowl, combine potatoes, carrots, olives, capers, olive oil, vinegar, salt, and pepper. Stir gently to combine. Fold in mayo. Make sure all ingredients are well coated. Refrigerate in sealed container overnight so flavors can blend.

The Feast of the Seven Fishes

The Feast of the Seven Fishes is an Italian–American holiday blowout based on Southern Italy's "La Vigilia," or Christmas Eve vigil. One must abstain from meat till Christmas Day, so fish it is! Why seven? It's possible the number refers to the seven hills of Rome. Most importantly, it's delicious. Here's my version of the clambake.

Smoked Salmon e Insalata Russa

Makes 12 servings

On an attractive platter, create a mound of Insalata Russa and surround with slices of smoked salmon, garnished with lemon zest and parsley. The appeal of the potato insalata is instead of peas it has briny capers to complement the smoked salmon, plus it gives your stomach a base for all the oily fish to come.

Insalata Russa (recipe: page 205)
16 ounces good quality smoked salmon
Grated zest of one lemon, for garnish
Minced parsley, for garnish

Tuna Casino on the Half Shell

Makes 12 servings

Pro Tip: 4-inch scalloped baking shells can be bought online.

5 slices thick-cut bacon, cut crosswise in ¼-inch strips
¼ cup red onion, minced
2 cloves garlic, minced
1 green bell pepper, minced
Juice of one lemon
2 pounds good quality fresh tuna, cut in 36 (¾-inch) chunks
Freshly ground pepper

Heat oven to 425°F. Spray 12 baking shells with cooking spray. Place on cookie sheets.

In medium skillet, over medium-high heat, cook bacon till slightly browned but not crisp, about 5 minutes. Set bacon aside, reserving one tablespoon fat in pan. Over medium heat, cook onion, garlic, and green pepper till softened, about 5 minutes. Return bacon to pan, add lemon juice, cook 2 minutes. Add freshly ground pepper to taste.

On 12 baking shells, place three pieces of tuna each. Spoon pan mixture gently onto each shell with tuna.

Bake 8 minutes till tuna is heated, serve immediately.

Crab Fra Diavolo

Makes 6 to 10 servings

4 tablespoons (½ stick) butter
5 cloves garlic, chopped fine
1 cup finely chopped sweet onion
1 pound fully cleaned crab, drained
Juice of one lemon
½ cup dry white wine
1 teaspoon dried oregano
1 teaspoon red chili flakes
1 can (28 ounces) diced tomatoes, drained
1 teaspoon salt
⅓ cup finely chopped parsley

In large pot, melt butter over medium-high heat. Add garlic and onion, cook till soft, about 4 minutes. Reduce heat to medium, add crab, lemon juice, cook stirring gently, 2 minutes. Add wine, oregano, red chili flakes, simmer gently till wine is reduced by half, about 5 minutes. Add tomatoes, salt, continue to simmer briskly 10 to 15 minutes till crab shreds, tomatoes soften and flavors meld. Mix in parsley, serve over 8 ounces cooked fettuccine.

Tomato Basil Baked Sardines

Serves 6 to 8

4 cans sardines (approx. 4 ounces each) skinless and boneless in oil
¼ cup olive oil, divided
1 large shallot, minced
2 cloves garlic, minced
16 ounces grape tomatoes, halved
¼ cup red wine vinegar
1 teaspoon freshly ground pepper
4 large leaves fresh basil cut in thin strips, divided

Heat oven to 350°F.

In a 9-inch round baking dish arrange sardines like the spokes of a wheel.

In medium skillet, heat 2 tablespoons oil over medium-high heat. Cook shallot and garlic till soft, about 4 minutes. Add tomatoes, vinegar, pepper, cook till tomatoes start to soften, 5 minutes. Stir in ½ basil.

Spoon tomato mixture over sardines, leaving parts of some fish exposed. Drizzle 2 tablespoons oil over tomatoes. Bake uncovered 20 minutes. Garnish with remaining basil and serve.

Fettuccine Puttanesca

5

Makes 12 servings

- 6 ounces dry fettuccine
- 2 tablespoons olive oil
- 2 cloves garlic, minced
- 6 anchovy fillets, rinsed, patted dry, chopped fine
- ½ cup pitted Kalamata or black olives, jarred not canned, chopped
- 2 tablespoons drained capers
- 1 can (14.5 ounces) plum tomatoes, coarsely chopped
- 1 teaspoon dried oregano
- ½ teaspoon red chili flakes
- ½ teaspoon salt
- Finely chopped fresh parsley, for garnish

In large pot, cook pasta in salted water till al dente. Drain, set pasta aside.

In pasta pot, over medium heat, add oil. When oil is shimmering, add garlic, anchovies. Mash anchovies into oil, cooking 5 minutes. Add olives, capers, cook 1 minute. Add tomatoes, oregano, chili flakes, salt. Simmer sauce gently, further breaking up tomatoes, 6 to 7 minutes.

Stir in pasta. Serve with parsley garnish.

Baked Cod with Artichokes and Sundried Tomatoes

6

Serves 4 to 8

- 2 (6-ounce) jars marinated artichoke hearts, drained and halved
- 1 (10-ounce) jar marinated sundried tomatoes, drained and cut in strips
- ½ cup pitted Kalamata or black olives, jarred not canned, chopped
- 2 cod fillets (2 pounds total) cut into 8 pieces
- Olive oil, for brushing fish
- ½ cup dry white wine
- Juice of one lemon
- 2 packed cups arugula, dressed in olive oil and balsamic vinegar
- Salt and freshly ground pepper

Heat oven to 350°F.

Coat a large baking dish with cooking spray. Arrange artichokes, tomatoes, and olives in dish, creating a "valley" in the center to place the fish. Season both sides of fish with salt and pepper. Set fish in center of vegetables. Brush fish with olive oil. Pour wine and lemon juice over fish.

Bake uncovered till fish flakes easily with fork, 25 to 30 minutes. Let rest for 10 minutes. Top with dressed arugula.

Shrimp Scampi

7

Serves 4 to 8

- 4 tablespoons (½ stick) butter
- 2 tablespoons olive oil
- 6 cloves garlic, minced
- ½ cup finely chopped red onion
- 28 large tail-on shrimp, peeled and deveined
- ¼ cup white wine
- 1 tablespoon lemon juice
- ½ teaspoon red chili flakes
- 1 teaspoon salt
- ⅓ cup chopped parsley

In large skillet, heat butter with the oil over medium heat. Add garlic and onion, cooking till soft, about 5 minutes. Add shrimp, stir to coat with butter mixture. Cook shrimp till they turn pink, about 4 minutes.

Add wine, lemon juice, red chili flakes, salt, and parsley, cook 2 minutes. Serve immediately over 8 ounces cooked fettuccine.

The Christmas Pork

Makes 8 servings

1 cup port wine

1 medium shallot, minced

¼ cup apple cider vinegar

1 tablespoon light brown sugar

2 cups dried apricots, divided

¾ cup dried cranberries

¾ cup pitted prunes

3 pound boneless pork loin roast, with a pocket for stuffing

1 stick butter, softened

4 cloves garlic, minced

2 tablespoons fresh thyme leaves

2 teaspoons salt

½ teaspoon cayenne

3 cups dried mixed fruit, soaked in ½ cup port and ½ cup
fresh apple cider till softened, about 20 minutes

Heat oven to 350°F and place rack in center.

In a small saucepan combine wine, shallot, vinegar, sugar. Bring just to a boil, reduce heat and simmer for 3 minutes to marry flavors. Let cool completely.

In another bowl combine apricots, cranberries, prunes. Stuff cavity of pork loin with fruit mixture.

Tie stuffed loin three or four times around with kitchen twine and place in roasting pan.

In a medium bowl, use fork to combine butter, garlic, thyme leaves, salt, cayenne. With hands, rub mixture over roast, coating liberally.

Pour wine mixture over loin. Place pan in center of oven. Roast 1 ½ to 1 ¾ hours. Baste meat with pan juices two or three times during roasting.

One hour after roast goes in oven, arrange the 3 cups marinated fruit including liquid to pan surrounding meat.

When interior of roast is at least 150°F remove from oven, let rest 20 minutes. Serve in ¾ to 1-inch slices, surrounded by the roasted fruit.

Ring-a-ling
Hear them ring
Soon it will be Christmas Day

Brussels Sprouts au Miel (with Honey)

Makes 6 servings

¾ cup dried cranberries	8 tablespoons peanut oil, divided
2 tablespoons honey	2 pounds Brussels sprouts
2 tablespoons apple cider vinegar	½ cup vegetable broth
¼ teaspoon cayenne pepper	2 large shallots, chopped fine
1 teaspoon salt	Freshly ground pepper

In small bowl, mix together cranberries, honey, vinegar, cayenne, and salt. Set aside.

Trim ends of sprouts, remove loose leaves, halve lengthwise. To a large nonstick skillet over medium-high heat add three tablespoons oil, heat till shimmering. Arrange one half sprouts in pan cut side down. Cook till browned and slightly softened, about 5 minutes.

Transfer sprouts to large bowl, set aside. Repeat with two tablespoons oil and rest of sprouts. Return first batch cooked sprouts to the pan.

Add vegetable broth to sprouts. Reduce heat to medium. Turn sprouts brown side up, cook till tender but still with a bit of crunch. Remove sprouts from pan and set aside.

Add another tablespoon oil to pan over medium-high heat and sauté shallots till soft and lightly browned, 3 minutes. Return sprouts to pan.

Add cranberry-honey mixture, remaining 2 tablespoons oil, 6 grinds black pepper and toss to combine.

Potatoes Au Gratin Suprême

Makes 8 to 10 servings

I use a food processor to slice the potatoes. Greatly speeds things.

7 tablespoons butter	½ teaspoon cayenne pepper
2 tablespoons all-purpose flour	3 pounds russet potatoes, peeled and
1 medium sweet onion, chopped fine	thinly sliced (6 to 9 potatoes) Keep
1 clove garlic, minced	in water so they don't turn brown.
2 cups half-and-half	2 cups shredded Gruyère (8 ounces)
2 tablespoons fresh thyme leaves	2 cups shredded Parmesan (8 ounces)
Salt and freshly ground pepper	

Heat oven to 350°F. Grease 9 by 13-inch baking dish with a tablespoon of butter and set aside.

In large skillet over medium-high heat melt 6 tablespoons butter. Add flour and whisk continuously till lightly colored, 3 to 5 minutes. Quickly add onion and garlic. Stirring with wooden spoon, lower heat to medium and cook till tender, about 3 minutes. Whisk in half-and-half, thyme, cayenne, 1 teaspoon each salt and pepper, simmer till mixture thickens slightly, 5 minutes.

Drain and dry potatoes well. Evenly layer half in baking dish and cover with half the cheeses. Pour half the wet mixture over this. Follow with remaining half potatoes, half the remaining cheese, the remaining wet mixture, end with the final quarter of cheese. Bake, uncovered, till top is golden, potatoes are easy to pierce with fork, about 1 hour. Rest 10 minutes before serving.

Sassy Red Cabbage

Makes 8 to 10 servings

1 medium red cabbage, about 3 pounds
6 tablespoons butter
1 large sweet onion, chopped fine
1 teaspoon ground cinnamon
1 teaspoon salt
1 teaspoon freshly ground pepper
2 Granny Smith apples, peeled, cored, cut in ½-inch cubes
½ cup good red wine
2 tablespoons sugar
2 tablespoons distilled white vinegar

Remove tough outer cabbage leaves, quarter, core, thinly slice, about ¼-inch, yielding about 15 cups.

In a large saucepan over medium-high heat, melt butter. Add onions, cook till softened, about 4 minutes.

To onions, add cabbage in batches, cook, stirring, till it collapses enough to make room for more. Add cinnamon, salt, and pepper, continue cooking, stirring constantly, till cabbage is shiny and fragrant, about 15 minutes.

Add apples, wine, stir. Reduce heat to medium, simmer, covered, till all is softened, 20 minutes more. Stir occasionally so cabbage doesn't stick. Just before serving, stir in sugar and vinegar.

Always Faithful Dinner Rolls

Makes 12 large rolls

5 tablespoons butter, divided	1 tablespoon active dry yeast
½ cup milk	1 teaspoon salt
2 tablespoons sugar	4 cups unbleached all-purpose flour

Using one tablespoon butter for each, generously coat a 9 x 13-inch baking dish, and a medium bowl for the dough to rise in.

In a small pot, melt 2 tablespoons butter, add milk, sugar, 1 cup water. Stir over medium-low heat till mixture reaches 103°F to 105°F. Liquid should be the temperature you'd like water to be for a hot shower. Pour liquid into a medium mixing bowl and sprinkle yeast on top. Whisk vigorously for a few seconds, cover with dark towel, let sit till foamy, about 5 minutes.

Add about two-thirds of the flour and all salt to bowl with yeast. With your hand, combine dry and wet ingredients to form dough. Incorporate remaining third of flour. Dough will start out shaggy and end a bit sticky. Knead for 4 minutes then transfer to buttered bowl, turning once to coat with butter. Cover bowl with dark towel and set in warm place till dough rises by about fifty percent, 30 minutes to an hour. Heat oven to 400°F. Punch dough down and divide into 12 balls. Pinch bottoms of balls together so tops are round. Place side by side in prepared baking dish. Cover with towel and let rise again in warm place, 15 minutes. Melt remaining 1 tablespoon butter and use to brush tops of rolls. Bake for 15 minutes or till tops are golden brown.

Figgy Pudding and Hard Sauce

We won't go until we get some
We won't go until we get some
We won't go until we get some
So bring it right here

FIGGY PUDDING

½ cup unsalted European-style butter, softened, plus more
    to grease mold
2 cups dried Turkish figs, stems removed and cut in eighths
1 cup dried cranberries
⅓ cup whiskey (whatever you got)
Juice of two oranges, about ¾ cup
Juice of one lemon
2 tablespoons grated orange zest
2 cups unbleached all-purpose flour
1 tablespoon arrowroot starch, or cornstarch
1 ½ teaspoons baking powder
¼ teaspoon baking soda
¾ cup brown sugar, firmly packed
¼ cup granulated sugar
1 ½ teaspoons ground cinnamon

½ teaspoon ground nutmeg
½ teaspoon ground ginger
½ teaspoon salt
2 large eggs
½ cup whole milk
¾ cup chopped walnuts

HARD SAUCE

½ cup (1 stick) butter, softened
2 cups confectioners' sugar
1 tablespoon lemon juice
1 teaspoon vanilla extract

In mixing bowl, beat butter, sugar, lemon juice, vanilla together till blended. Cover and chill 1 hour to meld flavors. Bring to room temperature 1 hour before serving.

Grease and flour 2-quart pudding mold or 2-quart metal bowl. Set aside.

In medium saucepan cover figs and cranberries with water, bring to boil over medium-high heat, reduce heat and simmer uncovered, 6 minutes. Drain.

In medium bowl, marinate figs and cranberries with whiskey, orange and lemon juices, and zest. Let sit for 15 minutes.

In mixing bowl whisk together flour, starch, baking powder, soda.

In stand mixer, or large bowl using hand mixer, cream together butter, 2 sugars, cinnamon, nutmeg, ginger, salt. Beat in eggs, one at a time.

Add flour mixture to butter mixture in three parts, alternating with milk, ending with flour, mixing till just combined. Drain fruit and add. Stir in walnuts.

Scoop batter into prepared mold or metal bowl. There should be at least an inch between top of batter and edge of mold. Grease lid of mold and cover, or use lightly greased aluminum foil secured firmly with string.

Into soup pot that can be covered, set wire rack or large metal jar lid. Place pot on stove. Place mold on rack in pot. Pour water halfway up side of mold. Over medium-high heat, bring water to boil. Reduce heat to a simmer, cover and steam for 2 to 2 ½ hours till a wooden skewer comes out clean. Add water as needed to maintain level.

Set serving plate upside-down on top of mold. Holding plate and mold together, invert, unmolding pudding onto serving plate.

Serve warm pudding topped with Hard Sauce.

Perfect Buckeyes

Makes 32 candies

A treasured Christmas treat at my house. My mom invented the skewer dipping method to keep the candies from having little chocolate skirts when you set them down to dry. Hence, perfect buckeyes! Warning: you may get a waistline like Santa if you eat too many of these. But they mean Christmas to me!

2 cups creamy peanut butter (I use Skippy)
¼ cup (½ stick) butter, softened
16 ounces confectioners' sugar
12 ounces semi-sweet chocolate chips

Equipment: three dozen 8-inch wooden skewers. Coffee cups and/or glasses as described

Line a baking sheet with parchment paper. In a roomy counter area, set out 6 to 8 coffee cups or heavy drinking glasses that are about 4 inches tall and 4 inches in diameter. More on these later.

In a large bowl, stir peanut butter and butter together thoroughly. Add sugar, continue stirring, then use your hands till all is fully combined. Shape into 1 to 1 ¼-inch balls by rolling between your palms. Place on the baking sheet, freeze for 45 minutes to an hour.

Use two pots similar in size, or a proper double boiler, for melting chocolate. Simmer 1 to 2 inches of water over medium to low heat in the bottom pot. Make sure bottom of top pot doesn't touch simmering water. Spray top pot with cooking spray before you add chocolate chips, for best cleanup. Melt chips and stir as needed till no lumps remain. Start this about ten minutes before peanut balls are finished firming up in the freezer.

Stick pointed end of an 8-inch wooden skewer into each chilled peanut butter ball then dip with a nice swirl so chocolate is about halfway up the side of each. Place the other end of your skewer in one of your cups so chocolate can harden. Depending on how heavy your cups or glasses are this may require some skillful balancing with multiple skewers to keep from tipping over a cup. Don't worry, it's not as hard as it might sound. I do all this by an open window in December in the Northeast to hasten chocolate hardening.

Running back and forth spearing them one at a time out of the freezer then running to dip them is what I do, but I don't recommend keeping your freezer door open for too long. As soon you're done dipping and all rested buckeye shells feel hard, remove each one from its skewer, close the hole in the peanut butter with your finger, and place (preferably uncovered) in fridge to firm up. Now don't eat 'em all in one sitting! Keep candies stored in fridge between servings.

Gingerbread Town

Makes 15 big ornaments

I dedicate this recipe to my mom, who was so creative at Christmas, and to my dad, who loved to make stained glass art. This "town" of house and building-shaped gingerbread ornaments couldn't be more fun to create. The look is a rustic, old country Christmas. The tinted "windows" and classic candies together are unique and charming. The recipe is simple, but you might find yourself (willingly) spending hours working on them because they're so entertaining to dream up. They last for weeks. The tree lights shining through the candy windows and the scent of gingerbread will add magic to every Christmas.

GINGERBREAD

½ cup sugar

½ cup shortening

½ cup unsulfured molasses

2 ½ cups all-purpose flour

1 tablespoon ground ginger

1 teaspoon ground cinnamon

½ teaspoon nutmeg

1 teaspoon baking soda

½ teaspoon salt

6 tablespoons water

1 bag (14 ounces) multi-colored Jolly Rancher candy

1 bag (13 ounces) Old Fashioned Classic Christmas Candy

ROYAL ICING

DO THIS LAST:

2 cups confectioners' sugar

¼ cup warm water

4 teaspoons light corn syrup

1 teaspoon vanilla extract

In medium bowl mix sugar and water. Add corn syrup and vanilla, stir thoroughly. Pipe cookies however you prefer and stick classic Christmas candies, candy canes, whatever you like, into the royal icing. Let cookies dry at room temperature for at least six hours, preferably overnight, before handling.

Heat oven to 350°F. In large bowl, with wooden spoon, mix sugar, shortening, molasses till well combined. In medium bowl, whisk together flour, cinnamon, nutmeg, ginger, baking soda, salt. Add one cup of flour mixture at a time, alternating with water, to form a soft dough. Add more water if dough is too dry.

Divide Jolly Ranchers by color and put in plastic bags. Put a dish towel down on the counter and with smooth side of a meat mallet give 'em a hammer till pulverized. You may need to double bag them, the shards can penetrate the plastic. Some remaining larger chunks are okay, they will melt in the process.

Take about ½ cup gingerbread dough, form in a ball, place between two sheets of parchment, roll out to ¼-inch thick.

Cover a baking sheet with parchment paper, spray with cooking spray. Roll out dough to about ⅓-inch thickness, envision then cut out your town's house and building shapes with a paring knife. Be sure to cut out windows. Don't cut into the kitchen counter or you will be in big trouble! Put down a cutting board if needed. Punch hole or holes with toothpick at top of each ornament to put clear cord or a hook through later on. Pick up scraps and return to gingerbread bowl. Dough will still be usable even if exposed to air for the whole time you're creating and baking. When ready, place cookies on prepared baking sheet and bake. After 5 to 7 minutes depending on thickness of gingerbread, put the crumbled hard candy in to fill the window openings (mix colors, go wild!), then bake 5 to 6 minutes more.

Let windows dry for about 10 minutes before trying to move. You will get the hang of how much crumbled Jolly Rancher candy to put in as you go. Keep re-spraying the parchment paper between batches. You may need to help the windows off the parchment with a spatula—once they are mostly dry they are pretty resilient. Follow icing recipe above right, to finish.

My infinite thanks, to . . .

Gray Coleman. My sun in the sky, my moon, my stars. Why this book exists.

My mamas, Helen and Bette, both my dear Grandmas, and ALL the ladies I love, both here and departed. How rich am I? They are my gold standard for ingenuity, skill, and inspiration.

Marco Marella. My Caravaggio, my Rembrandt, my Botticelli. Without you there is no light.

Dana Jacobi. For her linguistic dexterity, perseverance, and forever-upbeat spirit.

Tim Denbo. For his outstanding arrangements. **Joe McGowan.** For Tim.

Steven Yorra. My piano maestro and musical overlord. With love from the VOO Carré.

My sister, Kate. For life-saving recipe testing, photography, and essential moral support.

My culinary celebrities: Gabriele; Chef Billy; JoAnn; Chef Phillip; Tracie Griffin, Trevor Chase, & the Chase Family. Your humility from the mountaintop is an example for us all. **Michael Tapia.** For the introduction.

Gray Coleman. For celebrity interview editing. **Malachy Duffy.** For expert culinary encouragement.

Cathleen, Sharon, and Nina Rose Waters. Cathleen for French, Spanish, & Italian translations; Shar for following her own star; and Chef Nina for perfect Pizza Primavera, Focaccia, & Seven Layer Dip.

Angelique M. Rufty-Graux. For her native French language advice and her merveilleux sens de l'humour.

Mirian Rodriguez. For superhuman housekeeping during recipe testing. For two years, once a week, she turned a WWIII battlefield into a sparkling showplace. And **Roxana Soriano** for keeping my chalupas real.

Kelsey Whitsett, Natalia Pozzi, Gina Novak, and Karen Hinton. For endorsement connections, and faith.

All the folks at the International Culinary Center, and Vice Media Munchies. For the learnin' of a lifetime.

Ashley Graham & Ron Rona of Preservation Hall, Tom Cianfichi & Bryan Batt. For coming to my Monteleone ghost party, page 188. And **Bryan** for being my trusted Abigail Van Buren on matters large and small.

Kory Kirby. My design software savior. **Bonnie Slotnick.** For finding Dana. **Suzanne Fass.** Index goddess.

Dr. David Burrows, senior pastor, FBC, Las Cruces, NM. For scripture advice, Scripture Cake, pages 104-5.

Christopher Stroup. My April Showers cake princess, page 106. **Bahman Kalbasi.** For Persian perspicacity.

Denise Huddle. Arguably, my biggest fan. **Hope Bernhard.** Because what is life, without Hope?

All my taste-testers. For your courage. **Any dear friend who is not named here.** You know who you are.

Antoinette de Alteriis. For everything. And the great folks at Pelican and Arcadia for believing in me.

Jacques Pépin. For his uncommon kindness. **My Dad.** For always telling me: "You're a winner."

INDEX

Sei bravo. Dallo via.